END OF THE
TRAIL EATS

END OF THE TRAIL EATS

Cowboy-Approved Recipes from the Cowtown Cafe to the Saloon

NATALIE BRIGHT

TWODOT®

Essex, Connecticut
Helena, Montana

A · TWODOT® · BOOK

An imprint of Globe Pequot, the trade division of
The Rowman & Littlefield Publishing Group, Inc.
4501 Forbes Blvd., Ste. 200
Lanham, MD 20706
www.rowman.com

Distributed by NATIONAL BOOK NETWORK

British Library Cataloguing in Publication Information available

Library of Congress Cataloging-in-Publication

Names: Bright, Natalie, author.
Title: End of trail eats : cowboy-approved recipes from the cowtown café to the saloon / Natalie
   Bright.
Description: Essex, Connecticut : TwoDot, [2024] | Includes bibliographical references and
   index. | Summary: "A collection of 80 cowboy recipes from, featuring dishes from ranch
   kitchens, saloons, supply stations, cowtown cafes, and cook shacks. Includes archival photographs, Old West history, firsthand accounts, and profiles of the cooks who keep the traditions alive"— Provided by publisher.
Identifiers: LCCN 2023047051 (print) | LCCN 2023047052 (ebook) | ISBN 9781493076994
   (paperback) | ISBN 9781493077007 (epub)
Subjects: LCSH: Cooking, American—Southwestern style. | Cooking, American—Western style.
   | LCGFT: Cookbooks.
Classification: LCC TX715.2.S69 B74 2024 (print) | LCC TX715.2.S69 (ebook) | DDC
   641.5978—dc23/eng/20231206
LC record available at https://lccn.loc.gov/2023047051
LC ebook record available at https://lccn.loc.gov/2023047052

Dedicated to the people of the American West,
both past and present, from the urban dwellers to
the small-town folk, the dreamers, and the doers.
May our independence and grit endure.

Playing Faro in an Arizona saloon in 1895
Wikimedia

CONTENTS

"The Cow Boy" ca. 1888, Dakota Territory
Library of Congress

"Those were strenuous times, and we endured many hardships that
will never be recorded for the perusal of oncoming generations, but,
just the same, we had our day, and the world is better for it."

J. M. CUSTER, ALIAS BILL WILSON, TRAIL DRIVER

INTRODUCTION

Abilene, Kansas, was the first; Dodge City, the most famous and one that survived the longest, earning the tag "Cowboy Capital of the World." Ellsworth bragged about having the biggest stockyards. The deadliest, Newton. Wichita, Caldwell, Ogallala, and Ellis are worthy of mention as essential parts of the Kansas cattle trading center—a thriving business venture that spanned a time of just over thirty years or so, which is short, historically speaking, yet we still hold a fascination for what they accomplished.

An enterprising cowman from Illinois, Joseph McCoy, envisioned a place where the southern drover and the northern packing markets could meet. McCoy's instincts were right, and the Cowtown of Abilene was born.

Cowmen hired drovers to push their herds from their ranchlands in Texas northward to the railheads. Kansas city officials negotiated with railroad agents to fund construction of stockyards and telegraph services. Meat packers in Kansas City, St. Louis, and Chicago expanded their packing houses and sent representatives to negotiate with railroad agents and city councils. Stock buyers represented outfits from ranches who needed yearlings and seed stock to build their foundation herds. These buyers would often ride out to meet the trail bosses, and a deal would be cut before they had even reached the Cowtown stockyards.

All of these interests collided in Kansas.

What an experience it would have been for us Western enthusiasts to walk the streets of a Kansas Cowtown during those short decades following the Civil War. "We are here," wrote a *Dodge City Times* editor in 1885, "to live and get rich—if we can."

If you're imagining rowdy dusty cowboys and smelly longhorns, that's only half of it. While big money for cattle traders and packing houses was definitely the draw, other successful enterprises rode into town behind the dust of those hoof-beaten trails: saloon owners, runners and cappers (trail agents), bankers, liverymen, merchants, blacksmiths, lawyers, hotel proprietors, professional gamblers, good-time girls, and cooks.

The Cowtown saloons and hotel dining rooms became important business epicenters where cattle trading was negotiated. It was the innovative tavern owners who hired exceptional chefs, hosted events, employed professional gamblers to run exciting games, and hired beautiful "red-light gals." Proprietors claimed their share from liquor sales, dancing, gaming, and prostitution.

> "The average drive in a day was eight to ten and twelve miles, and the time on the trail was from sixty to ninety days, from points in Texas to Abilene or Newton, or Ellsworth, Kan."
>
> C. H. RUST, TRAIL DRIVER

Saloon interior
Panhandle-Plains Historical Museum, Canyon, Texas

Competition between communities was fierce as town councils planned events for the next season to entice drovers and purchased advertising in South Texas publications. Kansas newspaper editors were obviously loyal to their towns, working with city leaders to write articles bragging on the merits of their hotels, loading centers, and saloons while condemning the neighboring towns.

"They are, as a class, men, who make very little noise or show in the world, do their business on strictly business principles, and when their word is given it is just as good as their bond. That there are drovers who are unscrupulous and dishonest we admit; but they soon become known to the farmers and dealers, and it is only a question of a short time when they are compelled to seek some other business. There is no other business of the same extent that is so largely done 'on honor' as the livestock trade, and yet it is seldom that ever a dispute arises. Sales are made aggregating thousands of dollars, and although no papers are passed, the contract is always scrupulously carried out."

WILSON COUNTY CITIZEN, FREDONIA, KANSAS

On the one hand you had the trail-hardened cowboys just in from a five-month-long ride where they never abandoned the cattle in their charge. I think about those cowpunchers, perhaps too young of life's experience but long on skills. Loyal to the brand and dedicated to the work that had to be done, they hit town with a chance to relax and experience the pleasures of life. As young men in their late teens to mid-twenties, most of these drovers were unwed, seeking adventure with a reckless disregard for death. They hired on to ride a horse across thousands of miles to drive thousands of half-wild beasts and face every kind of danger you can imagine, from Mother Nature to cutthroat rustlers. Right after they hit Cowtown, they had pockets full of more cash than they had ever seen in their lifetime. A bath, clean duds, and a pair of shop-made boots were first on the agenda. Next came a stiff drink and something to eat besides beans and sourdough. Perhaps a dance or two with a willing partner; maybe something more.

The cattle-trailing wranglers included skilled livestock handlers of all skin color and background. A man's past did not matter. The color of a man's skin had no bearing on the skills, loyalty, and bravery he exhibited for the job. According to George W. Saunders, The Old Time Trail Drivers' Association founder, about one-third of the cowboys who went up the trail were Black or Mexican vaqueros.

Nothing like fine whiskey at the end of a long drive
Dodge City Times, July 17, 1880

Wranglers
Earn $30
Per Month
CATTLE DRIVE
Central Texas to
Montana Territory

~

Able to endure harsh
weather, hostile Comanches.

~

Dehorning & Animal
Doctoring Most Helpful

~

We do not care about a man's
Past, but require a good attitude.
Drinking, gambling, cussing
Will not be tolerated on trail.
Slaughter-Pecos Cattle Company

"From 1868 to 1895 it is estimated that fully 35,000 men went up the trail with herds, if the number of men computed by the number of cattle driven is correct. Of this number of men about one-third were negroes and Mexicans, another third made more than one trip."

GEORGE W. SAUNDERS, TRAIL DRIVER

Burrough Owens, Texas cowboy and cook with the 101 Ranch
Panhandle-Plains Historical Museum, Canyon, Texas

Historian Michael N. Searles acknowledges Mr. Saunders's observations and notes, "In 1860, slaves and free Blacks exceeded 30 percent of the Texas population with more than 83,000 people." He also points out that "the large number of cattle in Texas offered opportunities for enterprising men to turn a profit."

Outfits employed the revered Mexican vaquero. The skills they exhibited had been passed down for generations, long before the controlled northward migration of the Texas longhorns began. Many firsthand accounts pay tribute to these skills of the vaquero. Trail driver John James Haynes recalled, "During a storm we would ride among them, doing our best to get them settled, but in the darkness of the night, the blinding rain, loud peals of thunder, with vivid flashes of lightning to keep them excited, our efforts were often of no avail. When we saw that they were going, in spite of all we could do, we left two of our Mexican cowhands to 'tough it out' with them. No matter how many miles away we found the herd the next day, the faithful Mexicans were still with it."

On the other end of the spectrum opposite the Texas cowboys were the Eastern gentlemen, representing the railroads and the packing houses. They conducted business with the trail bosses and cattle barons while enjoying first-rate accommodations and dining. The stockyards and hotels wanted their return business, and unforgettable accommodations would offer one way of achieving that. What the trail-driving drover accomplished is remarkable, and I also think about the citizens who called a Kansas Cowtown home. The year-round residents had to prepare for thousands of visitors who returned every summer. They, to me, are the unsung stars we do not hear much about in this historic tale.

"Cow punchers" on horseback push livestock up a ramp and into a wooden train car
Cattle Raisers Museum, Fort Worth, Texas

The last of the herds would have shipped out late fall, October or early November. I can imagine that every family member breathed a sigh of relief when that final loaded livestock railcar pulled out of town. That break would have been short, though.

During the winter months town councils would begin making plans, running ads in Texas newspapers, and touting the reasons drovers should spend time in their town. Delegations would attend stock trader gatherings to rub elbows with the ranch owners and railroad agents. As A. J. Vanlandingham, commissioner of the Kansas City transportation bureau commented in his speech to the Cattle Raisers Association, "We handled last year over 394,000 cattle from Texas and the southern territory and are now first in receipts of Texas cattle." He added, "We think next to Fort Worth, Kansas City is the greatest city on earth."

Buyers look over a group of Texas Longhorns at the Great Union Stockyards, Chicago around 1900.
Library of Congress

"From Hannibal, Missouri, came the pine lumber, and from Lenape, Kansas, came the hard wood, and work began in earnest and with energy. In sixty days from July 1st a shipping yard, that would accommodate three thousand cattle, a large pair of Fairbank's scales, a barn and an office were completed, and a good three-story hotel well on the way toward completion."

JOSEPH G. MCCOY, CATTLE BARON

Back in Kansas, citizens were already preparing for the coming season. The tallgrass prairie is a well-watered, sweeping swath perfect for grazing herds. There are no trees for those wood burning stoves. Suppliers shipped goods west by rail, and those train cars returned east crammed with Texas longhorns.

As an old trailing cowboy Sam R. Riding observed, "Here along these trails passed the wealth of an empire." At its best there are numerous examples of supply meeting demand at rail shipping points. It is amazing what the citizens of these towns accomplished in such a short time. Texas and Kansas were bound in this venture, and the Kansas Cowtown imprinted its place in Western lore.

The variety of food in Cowtown is as diverse as the characters that walked along its streets. Oysters were a surprising item and very popular with diners. They arrived by train in large barrels of water or ice or were canned in small tins. While the tales of gunfights and cowboy mischief are certainly exciting, as I researched this book my curiosity always came back to the people who were assigned to the food preparation in the community. If you grew up in a family that involved work with long days of physical labor, as I did, you understand how much food these people can eat. Gathering around the table is not a culinary experience but a necessity that allows a body to wake up the next day at "can't see" and do what needs to be done. If it tastes good, and it usually does, that's a bonus.

Farming families began settling in the areas around Cowtown, which makes sense when you think about the flat, treeless land, perfect for the plow, and the produce needed to feed an influx of several thousand people. Corn, potatoes, beans, eggs, fresh milk, cream, and buttermilk would have to be furnished on a local basis in addition to needed foodstuffs brought by train.

The prep work for twenty-four-hour fine dining establishments must have been something to witness. Stacks of dirty dishes and piles of laundry were endless, I imagine, and it would have taken every single citizen, young and old, to ensure a successful cattle season. Families who called Cowtown home had a familiarity with hard work, and it did not deter them.

This collection of recipes reflects all the elements of Cowtown fare, including the history and firsthand accounts from the time period. From rib-sticking food to simple, delicious meals using basic ingredients that could be grown in local gardens, the results were oh so savory.

The resources for these dishes are varied, and I have included a few modern ranch recipes. I am a devoted recipe collector, but when it comes to cooking, I don't have a lot of time to prep, which is why I love the recipes in this book. Simple, easy, and full of flavor—just like the kinds of food our great-grandmothers might have prepared with ingredients they had on hand. When I cook cornbread in my grandmother's cast-iron skillet, I can imagine her watching over my shoulder, and the image of her placing a steaming square on my plate comes to mind.

Perhaps the flavor of these recipes will remind you of the hands that prepared the food before you. With each bite, you're getting a taste of the past.

The photographs included in this book span several decades. Although actual images from the early days of cow drives are extremely rare, you will recognize the work of the cowboy. The pride of community has not diminished, and the men on horseback exhibit a familiarity you will recognize. Cowboys still exist. Whether from 1880s or 2023, they rely on the same tools first used by the Mexican vaquero. The necessary skills needed to "make a hand" are crucial. "Makin' a hand" is the highest of compliments.

The age-old cowboy code of courage, loyalty to the brand, working without complaints, respect for women, and lack of curiosity about a man's past hold true in this century. There is pride in a job well done. I am privileged to

A cowboy stands on his horse in Newton, Kansas, early 1900s
Library of Congress

be around these kinds of people every day. Many other traditions continue as well, such as providing the outfit with a hearty meal. I can imagine how soul satisfying the home-cooked town food must have tasted to those saddle-weary cowpokes.

Lean, muscled cowboys with sweat-stained hats eased into Cowtown, where streets bulged with activity. The smells of dust and livestock were familiar to the cowboy, but as he tied up his horse and walked closer to the open door, he got a whiff of fresh rolls just out of the oven. The aroma almost brought him to his knees because it reminded him of home. Boots scuffled and spurs jangled as he and his friends took their seats. The menu was cluttered with fancy food, a real treat for men who didn't get their meals often enough to hurt their digestion.

THE NEW VENDOME
237 North Market Street, Wichita, Kansas
ᔆ
. . . DINNER . . .
Soup—Chicken Giglet, au Gratin. Radishes.
Sliced Tomato. Green Olives. Sweet Pickles.
Pommesa La Parisienne.
Dressed Lettuce with Eggs.
Roast Prime Rib of Beef, au jus.
Hamburger Roll, Tabasco Sauce.
New Potatoes in Cream.
Shrimp Salad.
Rhubarb Pie. Strawberries and Cream.
Assorted Cakes. Cream Cheese.
Water Crackers.
Hot Muffins.
Wheat, Rye or Graham Bread.
Tea. Coffee. Sweet Milk.
SUNDAY, MAY 15.
HASELWOOD, CHEF.
ᔆ
Meals 25 cents

At the table next to the trailing cowboys sat a handsome man in a dark suit, crisp white shirt, and thin necktie. He even had a pink wild prairie rose in his lapel. He greeted them with a toothy smile and extended an invitation for the boys to join him at the card table later. This professional gambler was instantly a best friend, but he thought nothing of taking every penny those cowpokes had. In a fair game, of course.

Several other tables scattered around the dining hall were full, where men with serious faces sat murmuring to one another. Perhaps railroad agents discussing stockyard expansion with city councils, or maybe packing house representative schmoozing cattle barons.

The merchants, carpenters, hotel maids, and their families all scrambled in from the busy street to eat as well. And what about those laborers who had an endless stream of train cars to unload, and then load again with bawling longhorns? Food had the power to bring all of these distinctly different individuals together. Food is community, because folks can't pursue their purpose if they're hungry.

In summation, I think vaudeville comedienne Eddie Foy describes the atmosphere of Cowtown the best in his memoir *Clowning Through Life*. Along with his acting partner, Jim Thompson, Foy had a highly successful two-season run in Dodge City.

I wish I could present to an audience of today an adequate picture of one of those old western amusement halls. Writers and artists have tried to do it, the movies have tried it, but all in vain—the sounds are lacking—the songs and patter from the stage at one end, where the show began at eight o'clock and continued until long after midnight; the click and clatter of poker chips, balls, cards, dice, wheels and other devices at the other end, mingled with a medley of crisp phrases— "Thirty-five to one!" "Get your money down, folks!" "Eight to one on the colors." "Keno!" "Are you all down, gentlemen? Then up she rises!" and a thousand other bits representing the numerous varieties of games that were being played, and which, though mostly spoken in a moderate tone, combined to make a babel of sound. All around the room, up above, a sort of mezzanine, ran a row of private boxes—and they were boxes, indeed! As plain as a packing case! Where one might sit and drink and watch the show. When the various stage performances were over, there was dancing which might last until four A.M. or daybreak.

Welcome to Cowtown.

Designed by Burgham and Root around 1875, the east limestone gate to the
Union Stock Yards in Chicago remains today.
Library of Congress

Cowboys, cattle, horses, and mules in West Texas
Cattle Raisers Museum, Fort Worth, Texas

INDIAN NATION

Trail bosses had much to consider when deciding on a route for walking their product to the railheads. For example, trails west out of Texas led to the quicksands and swift currents of the Pecos River. Cattleman Charles Goodnight declared it to be "the graveyard of the cowman's hopes" because he had lost too many valuable head during the crossing.

> "There were 500 Indians camped near the trail, and nearly every herd that passed gave them beef. Hundreds of cowboys knew Quannah Parker, and he had scores of friends among the white people."
>
> T. J. BURKETT SR., TRAIL DRIVER

Quanah Parker, Comanche Indian Chief
Library of Congress

All hoof-hardened paths north encountered the Red River. A shift towards the east and then north pushed drovers to confrontation with jayhawkers, bands of rustlers and robbers that ruled parts of Kansas. Bandits were not afraid to take on the hot-blooded cowboys who were bent on getting their herds to market. Conflict did not deter either side.

After crossing the Red, directly north lay Indian Nation.

In 1829 President Andrew Jackson requested legislation to relocate five tribes of Native Americans who lived in the South. He called for "an ample district west of the Mississippi . . . to be guaranteed to the Indian tribes as long as they shall occupy it."

Most of central and southern Mississippi, a land of moss-covered forests and clear streams, was settled by the Choctaw Nation. The Cherokee Nation had called parts of Georgia, North Carolina, Tennessee, and Alabama home for generations. The Chickasaw people claimed the thick timber areas of northern Mississippi and parts of Tennessee and northwestern Alabama. Mangrove forests and wetlands of the Florida Everglades provided a home to the Seminoles. The Creek lived on the flatlands of Alabama and Georgia.

Generations of First Americans had lived in these areas, where they had established homes and farms, growing crops and raising livestock.

Various treaties and payments were initiated. President Jackson ordered strict enforcement, and the Choctaws were removed first, beginning in 1831. The Cherokees received $5 million in exchange for their seven million acres of ancestral homelands, and the military was ordered to evict them at gunpoint and force their journey westward. The remaining tribes followed. The route they walked, twelve hundred miles, which took six months, is known as the Trail of Tears. Adding to the tensions was the Cherokees and Choctaws' participation in the War of 1812, a service that President Jackson seemed to have overlooked. Forced treaties, illegal enforcement, and conflict within and among the tribes ultimately led to the removal of the southeastern tribes to land out west.

The claimed reasoning for the relocation is that they would have a guaranteed homeland and could develop and build on their own, retaining their culture without the influence of others. Also, Jackson believed that a nation could not exist within a nation. Their new home was the plains area in what is now Oklahoma. Incidentally, White settlers were already there.

Over the decades, it became known as Indian Country, then Indian Territory, a land crisscrossed by the boundaries of multiple tribal nations and reservations.

From the time the great livestock movement began and crossed the Red River, the trail drivers passed through Indian Nation. The migration of Texas longhorns that started in 1866, however, brought significant numbers of livestock and people that could not be ignored—not only the Texas cattle but also an unbelievable number of immigrants. An estimated twelve million European immigrants arrived in the United States between 1870 and 1900, led by Ireland, Germany, Great Britain, Canada, France, Switzerland, Mexico, Norway, the Netherlands, and Italy. Chinese had already settled in California during the gold rush by the time herds moved northward. This incursion into the native peoples' established hunting grounds was endless.

A few passing through could be tolerated, but allowing hundreds of thousands of cattle was too much to ask. On occasion trail drivers were met by delegations of braves from various tribes, who requested a toll of ten cents per head. Some of the tribes laid out a defined route. The alternate route east put them up against fierce opposition from Kansas and Missouri farmers over the ticks that Texas longhorns were immune

> "[C]rossing Red River out by Carriage Point, by way of Fort Arbuckle into Indian Territory, out by Oswego, Kansas. Here we met a bunch of friendly Comanche Indians who had been out on the banks of the Arkansas River making a treaty with another tribe."
>
> LEO TUCKER, TRAIL DRIVER

> "We were on the Chisholm Trail in the Indian Nation, and on the Wichita River some Indians came to us and wanted us to give them some cattle for allowing us to pass through their country. We gave them a few lame cows, and they never bothered us anymore."
>
> A. F. CARVAJAL, TRAIL DRIVER

against but caused a fatal Spanish fever in other breeds. For the sake of time, most trail bosses met the requirements of the tribes to keep the herds moving.

C. F. Doan had lived near Cache Creek and Fort Sill, Oklahoma, where he processed beef for the Indian tribes and later, while living at Doan's Crossing, would save parts of butchered beeves for Quanah Parker. In an interview, Doan's daughter, Bertha Doan Ross, recalls how proud her father was of the native name they had given him. It was years later that Doan discovered the translation: Chief Gut Man. In his memoirs written for the Trail Drivers Association, Doan often expressed concern that the rations provided to the tribes were never enough. He observed, "After the bi-weekly killings, the Indians would feast and sing all night long and eat up their rations and nearly starve until the next issue day came."

The endless numbers of free-range cattle offered opportunities for all. Some tribal members built cattle ranches, like Montford Johnson, the well-known Chickasaw cattleman who lured unbranded wild cattle into holding pens by offering salt licks.

> "Saunders offered to make settlement by given them one horse and some provisions, and the Indians seemed well pleased with this offer. When we started our herd, about twenty young bucks riding on beautiful horses came and helped us swim the cattle across the Canadian River."
>
> T. T. HAWKINS, TRAIL DRIVER

Despite the hardships and broken spirits, the tribes persevered and continued to celebrate their unique cultures through song and dance in a spirit of tradition and hope for the future.

> "A few days later as we were traveling along we saw ahead of us something that looked like a ridge of timber, but which proved to be about four hundred Comanches who were coming our way. They were on the warpath and going to battle with another tribe. When they came up to our herd they began killing our beeves without asking permission or paying any attention to us. . . . They killed twenty-five of our beeves and skinned them right there, eating the flesh raw and with blood running down their faces."
>
> L. D. TAYLOR, TRAIL DRIVER

Old-Fashioned Fry Bread

Authentic fry bread would have been lard and flour, the only provisions available from the provided government rations. Each tribe added its own twist to the basic recipe.

Yield: 16–20 servings

Ingredients:
4 cups flour
2 tablespoons baking powder
1 teaspoon salt
½ cup shortening
1 cup warm water

> Everyone was welcome at Cow Camp. "Eight to ten Indians frequently would come up just about time for dinner, and I would always have our cook, a white boy, prepare lots of food and we would fill the Indians up."
>
> JAMES MARION GARNER,
> TRAIL DRIVER

Directions:

Mix flour, baking powder, and salt. Gradually add the shortening and water, adding only enough water to make the dough stick together. Knead dough until smooth. Form into fist-sized balls, cover them with a towel for 10 minutes, then pat them out into circles about the size of a pancake. Fry in hot cooking oil in cast-iron skillet until brown on both sides. Drain on paper towels.

Cherokee Fry Bread

Yield: 6 servings

Ingredients:
1 cup flour
½ teaspoon salt
2 teaspoons baking powder
¾ cup milk

Directions:

Mix ingredients, adding more flour if necessary, to make a stiff dough. Roll out the dough on a floured board till very thin. Cut into strips, 2 x 3 inches, and drop in hot cooking oil. Brown on both sides. Serve hot with honey.

Chickasaw Fry Bread

Yield: 8 servings

Ingredients:

2 cups sifted flour

½ teaspoon salt

4 teaspoons baking powder

1 egg, beaten

½ cup warm milk

Directions:

Stir first three ingredients together, then stir in the beaten egg. Add milk to make a soft dough. Place dough on a floured breadboard; knead lightly. Roll dough out to ½ inch thick. Cut into strips, 2 x 3 inches, and slit the center. Drop strips into hot cooking oil and brown on both sides. Serve hot.

Creek Fry Bread

Yield: 8 servings

Ingredients:

2 cups flour

1 tablespoon baking powder

¼ teaspoon salt

1 cup buttermilk

Directions:

Sift flour, baking powder, and salt. Add milk and enough additional flour, if needed, to make a stiff dough. Roll out onto floured breadboard and cut into 4 x 4-inch squares with a slit in the center. Fry in hot cooking oil until golden brown. Drain on plate with paper towels.

ARBUCKLE'S
AXLE GREASE

Arbuckle Ariosa brand coffee was the brand most used on the range. "Axle grease" refers to the strength of the coffee.

Coffee

Yield: 1 serving

Ingredients:

½ teacup Ariosa coffee, ground

5–6 teacups boiling water

Directions:

Stir coffee into boiling water. Boil for 20 minutes. Remove from fire. Add ¼ teacup cold water and let stand for 1 minute.

Arbuckles' Ariosa coffee advertisement,
The Aegis & Intelligencer, February 1907
Wikimedia

You get a heaping pound of the pure old-fashioned Arbuckles' ARIOSA Coffee, that took care of the nerves and digestion of your grandparents, and has been the leading coffee of the world for 37 years.

You'll never have to <u>quit</u> drinking Arbuckles.'

Don't let any man switch you over to coffee that pays him big profits at the expense of your heart, stomach and nerves.

Complies with all requirements of the National Pure Food Law, Guarantee No. 2041, filed at Washington.

When John Arbuckle developed a way to preserve roasted coffee beans,
his brand became the only drink trailing cowboys knew.
Natalie Bright

A Texas longhorn in his pen, the Stockyards district of Fort Worth, Texas
Library of Congress

"In the fall of 1867, my father, my oldest brother, and myself, with three other hands, left Palo Pinto with 900 steers, our destination being Shreveport, Louisiana."

WILLIAM BAXTER SLAUGHTER, TRAIL DRIVER

CHAPTER 1

BREAKFASTS AND BREADS

"A little flame is seen flickering in camp, and the cook's call is heard, 'Roll out!' You jump up, but before you have time to dress and pack your bed the second call is heard, 'Breakfast!'"

HOLM DODSON, TRAIL DRIVER

Ham and Red Eye Gravy

An easy use of pan drippings that adds exceptional flavor to cured ham and potatoes. Good for any meal any time of the day, but especially filling for breakfast when served with hot biscuits.

Yield: 1 ham slice per person

Ingredients:
Cured country ham, sliced about ¼ inch thick
1 tablespoon butter or other fat
Reserved pan juices from frying the ham
½ cup strong black coffee
⅓ cup hot water, if needed
Black pepper, to taste
Worcestershire sauce, as desired

Directions:

Make a cut in the layer of fat around the ham about every 3 inches. This will help keep the ham slice from curling badly while it cooks. (Some people like to remove the "rind," or outer skin layer, from the ham prior to cooking.) In a large skillet or cast-iron frying pan, melt the butter or other fat. Add the ham slice and fry, turning ham after about 2 minutes; let it cook until the fat around the edge is translucent and the ham is golden. Do not overcook the ham. Remove ham from the pan and set aside; keep warm in a low-temperature oven.

For Red Eye Gravy: Deglaze frying pan with the coffee, scraping all bits and pieces loose from the bottom of the pan. (**Note:** Some ham may be too dry to have any pan juices after frying. In this case, before adding the coffee, add ⅓ cup hot water. Then add the coffee to do the deglazing.) Increase heat to high and let mixture boil approximately 2–3 minutes, or until reduced in half and thickened. Season with pepper and Worcestershire to taste.

Pour Red Eye Gravy over cooked ham slices. Serve with fried or mashed potatoes, fried eggs, grits, and biscuits if you like.

Two British chemists, John Lea and William Perrins, invented Worcestershire sauce in the 1830s in Worcester, England, for a customer who never returned to claim the product. The aged and bottled sauce reached America around 1840.

Cowman's Omelet

Simple, easy one-pan breakfast.

Yield: 6 servings

Ingredients:

6 slices bacon, diced
2 tablespoons finely chopped onion
1 cup grated potato
6 large eggs, slightly beaten
½ teaspoon salt
Black pepper, to taste
Dash of hot sauce [page 90]
2 tablespoons minced parsley

> "There were no fences—the range was open from the Gulf of Mexico to North Dakota as far as I went."
>
> E. P. BYLER, TRAIL DRIVER

Directions:

Fry bacon until crisp; remove from pan and drain, leaving at least 2 table-spoons of bacon grease in pan. Add onion and sauté over low heat until soft. Add grated potato and cook until light brown. Mix together eggs, salt, pepper, and hot sauce; pour into pan. As omelet cooks, lift up edges with spatula to allow egg mixture to slide under. When firm, sprinkle omelet with crumbled crisp bacon and parsley. Fold over and serve.

Modern day cowboys at the Sanford Ranch, Texas
Natalic Bright

Egg Casserole

Nothing like a tasty, easy breakfast casserole. Older recipes call for lots of onion, which you can adjust according to your taste.

Yield: 10 servings

Ingredients:

1 pound sausage, cooked and drained

4 large onions, diced

12 slices white bread, quartered

3 cups grated cheddar cheese

8 eggs, beaten

4 cups milk

¼ teaspoon sugar

½ teaspoon dry mustard

"Timid men were not
among them—the
life did not fit 'em."
CHARLES GOODNIGHT

Directions:

Sauté onion in sausage drippings until soft. Place one-half of the bread in the bottom of a greased 9 x 13-inch pan. Sprinkle one-half the sausage, onions, and cheese on the bread; repeat these layers. Combine eggs, milk, sugar, and dry mustard; pour over top layer. Refrigerate for at least 24 hours before cooking. Remove from refrigerator 1 hour before baking. Bake at 350°F for 45–50 minutes.

As fresh milk sits undisturbed, cream rises to the top. The cream is placed in a jar with wooden paddles and stirred vigorously, resulting in butter. The liquid left in the churn after the butter is removed is buttermilk. Adding vinegar or lemon juice to cream results in sour cream.

South Dakota Farm Pancakes

Using simple, fresh ingredients a farmhouse would keep on hand, serve these pancakes for a genuine country breakfast topped with an easy strawberry sauce. You might have noticed that older recipes included "sift the flour" in the instructions. I remember watching my grandmother doing this, particularly for cakes. Today's flour is finer and clump-free; no sifting required.

Yield: 4–6 pancakes

Ingredients:

¾ cup flour

1 tablespoon sugar

1 cup sour cream

4 eggs

1 cup small curd cottage cheese

Directions:

Sift flour and sugar into mixing bowl. Blend in sour cream. In a separate bowl, beat eggs until light and fluffy. Fold into flour-sugar-sour cream mixture along with cottage cheese. Cook each side on a greased griddle until golden brown. Top with hot melted butter and warm strawberry sauce (recipe below).

Easy Strawberry Sauce

Yield: About 1½ cups

Ingredients:

1 pound strawberries, rinsed and thinly sliced

⅓ cup sugar

1 tablespoon lemon juice (from ½ lemon)

Directions:

In medium saucepan, combine sliced strawberries, sugar, and lemon juice. Place over medium heat and bring to a boil, stirring occasionally. Strawberries will release juice without any mashing required. Reduce heat and simmer 20–30 minutes, or until sauce is thickened, stirring occasionally. Remove from heat. ***Note:*** The sauce will thicken as it cools, even more when refrigerated.

Fluffy Pancakes

From the award-winning chuck wagon cooking team of the Wild Cow Ranch run by Shirley and Don Creacy, this basic recipe results in a light and fluffy hotcake. The perfect start to a day in the saddle.

Yield: 6 (4½-inch) perfect pancakes

Ingredients:

1 egg
¾ cup plus 2 tablespoons milk
2 tablespoons oil
1 cup flour
½ teaspoon salt
2 tablespoons baking powder
2 tablespoons sugar

Directions:

Mix dry into wet ingredients with a whisk or fork. Preheat griddle; lightly grease before adding batter. Cook pancakes on both sides. Top with butter and warmed maple syrup.

"The prairies near Abilene, Kansas, where we held our herds, were partly taken up by grangers, who lived in dugouts, a square hole in the ground, or on the side of a bluff. . . . The grangers were active among the herds, asking the cattleman to bed cattle on their lands so they could use the chips for fuel. . . . The grangers figured that 1,000 cattle would leave chips on the ground in one night to give them 500 pounds of fuel in a few days."

GEORGE W. SAUNDERS, TRAIL DRIVER

Cowboys on horseback on the range, chuck wagons in background, Utah or Colorado, dated 1905
Library of Congress

Breakfasts and Breads 7

SINGING COWBOYS: TRUTH OR LEGEND?

The legend of the singing cowboy is true. Trail-driving wranglers really did sing to the herds at night. The rhythmic melody often reflected the gait of the horse the wrangler rode as he sang about his life and troubles as a working cowboy. His experiences became songs. The vaquero brought tunes with joyful, hard-driving rhythms from below the Rio Grande, while the Black cowboys sang the ballads and minstrels of their heritage. The melodies of popular church hymns brought memories of home. Often the altered words, while clever and comical, would never be repeated within earshot of the womenfolk. They sang of stampedes, outlaws, bronc busting, romance, and death.

> "Many is the time I have listened to the chant of the night songs as the boys went around the herd."
>
> I. H. ELDER, TRAIL DRIVER

The origins of one favorite song can be traced to 1873 Kansas. "Home on the Range" became extremely popular with drovers. Frontier physician and homesteader Dr. Brewster Higley shared his poem "Western Home" with friends, who encouraged him to publish it. Former army bugler Daniel E. Kelley set the words to music. As its popularity grew, the song became known under various titles. First released in sheet music in 1925, the familiar words "Oh give me a home" rose in popularity again in 1933 when Bing Crosby recorded the song with his orchestra. In 1947 "Home on the Range" became the official state song of Kansas.

Another favorite with cowboys, "The Old Chisholm Trail" has a catchy, lively verse that pairs well with a trotting horse. Through the years, as its popularity grew with the outfits drifting north and the cowboy culture in general, the song gathered hundreds of stanzas. Corwin Doan operated a trading post at the popular crossing near the Red River on the Western Trail and recalls: "Here, my old adobe house and I sit beside the old trail and dream away the days thinking of the stirring scenes enacted when it seemed an endless procession of horses and cattle passed, followed by men of grim visage but of cheerful men, who sang the 'Dying Cowboy' and 'Bury Me Not on the Lone Prairie' and other cheerful tunes as they bedded the cattle or, when in a lighter mood, danced with the belles of Doan's or took it straight over the bar of the old Cow Boy saloon."

> "When the cattle are restless on the bedding ground, the boys on night herd hum a low, soft lullaby (like a mother to her child). It has a quieting effect and often saves trouble."
>
> JOHN C. JACOBS, TRAIL DRIVER

The Old Chisholm Trail
Come 'long, boys, and listen to my tale
I'll tell you of my troubles on the old Chisholm trail.
Coma ti yi youpy, youpy ya, youpa ya
Coma ti yi youpy, youpy ya.

Square dances, community hoedowns, Wild West shows, and country bands kept the tunes of the cowboy vibrant. With its debut in the 1920s, radio brought a new fan base of families who listened to the old trail songs. One such radio performer with the NBC station in New York City was John I. White. He began collecting and learning the songs of the range cowboys after visiting cousins in Arizona. By the turn of the twentieth century, long after the end of the trailing days, the cowboys' songs gained attention and Hollywood caught

> **"Gus Staples, one of our boys, was a fiddler, and we had music all the way."**
> R. J. JENNINGS, TRAIL DRIVER

the buzz. The 1933 western movie *Riders of Destiny* featured the character Singing Sandy Saunders, played by a young John Wayne outfitted in a black ten-gallon hat. His singing voice was reportedly dubbed. We are thankful that John Wayne followed the path of acting, while other successful careers emerged for the white-hatted heroes who could ride and actually sing.

Radio and then television launched the career of "Oklahoma's Singing Cowboy." Gene Autry began performing on radio station KVOO in Tulsa, realizing much success thanks to the Sears, Roebuck and Co. catalog, which featured his music and a $9.95 Gene Autry Grand Concert guitar. It came with strings, a pick, and two books, *The Art of Writing Songs* and *How to Play the Guitar*. For only $12.95, your order would include an artificial leather case.

Hollywood came calling soon after. Republic Pictures featured Autry in *Tumbling Tumbleweeds*, which grossed more than $1 million, making him a cowboy singing sensation. There was no turning back—Autry appeared in a total of ninety-three films.

Gene Autry
Wikimedia

Herb Jeffries
Wikimedia

A series of all-Black singing cowboy movies was produced between 1936 and 1939 starring Herb Jeffries. A jazz vocalist, Jeffries determined that Black youth needed a cowboy hero too and approached independent producer Jed Buell to help make the idea a reality.

Several other well-known performers got their start on radio: Rex Allen from Arizona, Tex Ritter from Houston, and a young actor named Roy Rogers who performed with a singing trio he helped bring together, the Sons of the Pioneers. Dubbed the "King of Cowboys," Rogers appeared in more than one hundred films along with his equally famous palomino horse, Trigger, the "Smartest Horse in the Movies."

Helen Parrish, Roy Rogers on Trigger, and George "Gabby" Hayes in *Sunset Serenade*
Wikimedia

"Often I have taken my old fiddle on herd at night when on the trail, and while some of my companions would lead my horse around the herd I agitated the catguts. . . . And say, brothers, those old long-horned Texas steers actually enjoyed that old time music."

LAKE PORTER, TRAIL DRIVER

Thanks to the technology of today, we can enjoy many of these old movies. And thanks to several organizations such as the Western Writers of America and events like Elko, Nevada's National Poetry Gathering, the work, hardships, and dreams of the American cowboy are kept alive in prose, song, and verse.

Playbill for *Along the Navajo Trail* starring Roy Rogers, Dale Evans, and Estelita Rodriguez
Wikimedia

Cheyenne Scrapple

Credited to a cook at the Steer Head Saloon & Café in Cheyenne, Wyoming, this recipe is dated late 1800s. Most often served at breakfast, scrapple is a way of using leftover pork such as loin ends and rib tips, holding true to the frontier concept of "head-to-tail" use of a butchered hog. The authentic dish used a variety of organ meats, which were boiled with spices and vegetables, and there are numerous versions. November 9th is National Scrapple Day. Season to your preference, as there are no seasoning measurements provided in this authentic recipe.

Yield: 8–12 servings

Ingredients:
3 pounds pork sausage, crumbled
3 quarts water
1 pound beef liver (optional)
Dried parsley
Sage
Poultry seasoning
Salt
Cornmeal

Directions:

Boil pork sausages in 3 quarts of water. Add beef liver, if desired. Cook until meat is well done. Add dried parsley, sage, poultry seasoning, and salt. Stir moistened cornmeal into meat broth until thickened. Spoon into five loaf pans; refrigerate. Slice when cold into thin slices and put on a baking sheet in 375°F oven, turning once. Bake to a delicate crispness. Can also be fried in a cast-iron skillet or on a griddle with butter. Serve with cinnamon rolls, fresh sliced tomatoes, and apple butter, honey mustard, or maple syrup. Try it mixed with scrambled eggs.

"After thirty years of settled life the call of the trail is with me still, and there is not a day that I do not long to mount my horse and be out among the cattle."

L. B. ANDERSON, TRAIL DRIVER

Roundup Scrapple

It's interesting that I find most authentic scrapple recipes listed under the breakfast section, maybe because most of the older recipes call for "pork scraps." In some areas the traditional dish uses oats or buckwheat flour instead of cornmeal. This interesting version combines both beef and pork that cooks up crispy on the outside and soft in the center.

Yield: 6 servings

Ingredients:
½ pound ground beef or pork, or combination
1 medium onion, chopped
Lard or bacon grease
1 teaspoon salt
⅛ teaspoon pepper
1¼ cups water
1 cup cornmeal

Directions:

Brown meat and onion slowly in a bit of leftover bacon grease or other fat. Add seasonings and water. Cook over low heat 20 minutes. Slowly stir in cornmeal and cook 4–5 minutes. Turn into loaf mold and cool. Cut into slices and fry in hot fat until brown. Serve with gravy.

Roundup scenes on Belle Fouche [*sic*] in South Dakota, 1887
Library of Congress

Corn Breakfast Muffins

Dated 1919, this is one example of many recipes from the American West that use cornmeal. This easy recipe is reprinted here as it appeared in the *Grand Forks Herald*. A "quick oven" is translated to 425°F. Something so simple is packed with flavor. Time to rise and shine.

Directions:

To the yolks of three eggs, beaten very light, add two cupfuls buttermilk; sift into this one cupful and a half of white corn meal, half a cupful of flour, soda, salt, and baking powder (one teaspoonful of each), and two teaspoonfuls of sugar. Then stir into two tablespoons of melted butter. Pour into greased and smoking hot muffin rings and bake in a quick oven [425°F] for 15 minutes.

Author's note: Muffin rings are circular-shaped and would have been placed on a cast-iron griddle or skillet. I used a muffin pan coated with nonstick cooking spray. A cast-iron gem pan or wedge pan would work as well. Be sure to preheat your cast-iron pan before pouring in the batter. These muffins are light and flavorful, a morning treat when drizzled with honey and enjoyed with a cup of coffee.

Frontier Oven Temperature Guide
Very slow oven = 275°F
Slow oven = 325°F
Moderate oven = 375°F
Hot or quick oven = 425°F

Easy Corn Bread

Corn bread is listed on menus from Chicago to St. Louis and, of course, throughout the Midwest. There are certain truths that apply to corn bread. Number one: The most delicious results come from bacon grease, the kind that comes from the jar on the stove. Number two: Your best cast-iron skillet will ensure the best outcome. The age-old debate of sugar or no sugar—that's for you to decide.

Yield: 2–4 servings

Ingredients:
2 tablespoons bacon drippings
1 cup white cornmeal
1 teaspoon baking powder
1 teaspoon salt
1 large egg, lightly beaten
1 cup buttermilk (more if needed)

Yes, we'll come to the table as long as we're able, and eat every damn thing that looks sorta stable.

Directions:

Place 1 tablespoon bacon grease in a 6½-inch skillet; place skillet in the oven while it preheats to 425°F. Whisk together the cornmeal, baking powder, and salt in a small bowl. Whisk together the egg, buttermilk, and remaining bacon drippings in a medium bowl. Add the dry ingredients to the buttermilk mixture and stir just until combined. (The mixture should be the consistency of pancake batter. If too dry, add more buttermilk.) Pour the batter into the hot skillet. Bake until the crust is dark golden brown, 15–20 minutes.

"This was my first trip as a cow puncher, and when we reached Red River a lot of Indians came and stayed with us all day. To me, a beardless boy, those Indians in the war paint was a wonderful sight."

B. D. SHERRILL, TRAIL DRIVER

Sour Cream Corn Bread

The addition of cream-style corn and sour cream turns this from a pan of ordinary corn bread to extraordinary. The only problem is what to serve it with. Pot of beans, boiled cabbage, chili, beef stew? Yes.

Yield: 8 servings

Ingredients:

½ cup vegetable oil (substitute bacon grease for more flavor)

1 cup sour cream

1 (8-ounce) can cream-style corn

3 large eggs, lightly beaten

1 cup self-rising white cornmeal mix

¼ teaspoon salt or seasoned salt, or to taste

Directions:

Pour ¼ cup oil into a 9-inch cast-iron skillet. Place the skillet in the oven while it preheats to 400°F. In a large bowl, combine the remaining ¼ cup oil, the sour cream, corn, eggs, cornmeal mix, and salt until well blended. Pour the hot oil from the skillet into the batter; stir to combine. Pour the batter into the hot skillet and bake until the top is lightly browned, about 45 minutes.

"How dear to my heart are the scenes of my trailhood, when fond recollections present them to view—the water barrel, the old chuck wagon, and the cook who called me to chew."

T. T. HAWKINS, TRAIL DRIVER

Sweet Onion Corn Bread

Large and sweet onions fresh from the field would be perfect.

Yield: 8 servings

Ingredients:

2 cups self-rising white cornmeal mix
1 tablespoon sugar
1 teaspoon baking powder
2 cups milk
2 tablespoons oil or bacon drippings
1 large egg, lightly beaten
2 cups finely chopped sweet onion

Directions:

Preheat the oven to 350°F. Grease a 9-inch cast-iron wedge pan. In a large bowl combine the cornmeal mix, sugar, baking powder, milk, oil, and egg until well blended (the batter will be thin). Add onions, stirring until well blended. Pour the batter into the prepared pan and bake until golden brown, about 40 minutes. Let cool before serving.

Cowboys from the XIT Ranch in the Texas Panhandle eat at the chuck wagon.
Library of Congress

Cowtown Rolls

The Fleischmann's brand of dry yeast is the country's oldest baker's yeast, first introduced to US cooks around 1868 by Austrian brewers Charles and Maximilian Fleischmann. This new convenience offered a quick and easy alternative to the attention required to maintain an active sourdough starter. You may have noticed that older recipes are not as detailed in instruction as today, but you can use your best judgment as to how long "a little while" might be after you "make into rolls." You can do this.

Yield: 12 rolls

Ingredients:
2 packages dry yeast
2 cups warm water
2 cups flour
⅓ cup oil
⅓ cup sugar
1 egg, beaten
2 teaspoons salt
4–5 cups flour

Directions:

Dissolve yeast in warm water. Combine the first 2 cups flour, oil, sugar, egg, and salt; stir. Add 4–5 cups flour and mix. Let rise at least 25 minutes. Make dough into rolls; allow to rise a little while. Bake at 400°F for 15–20 minutes.

Feet in the stirrups and seat in the saddle,
I hung and rattled with them long-horned cattle.

Old-Fashioned Biscuits

There is nothing like a quick and easy baking powder biscuit with butter and jelly to start the day. This easy basic recipe has been around for generations.

Yield: 18 (2-inch) biscuits

Ingredients:
2 cups flour
4 teaspoons baking powder
1 teaspoon salt
3 tablespoons shortening
¾–1 cup milk

His coffee tasted
like water scalded
to death.

Directions:

Preheat oven to 450°F. Sift together flour, baking powder, and salt. Cut in shortening until like coarse crumbs; add milk and mix lightly to make a soft dough. Knead lightly on floured surface and roll dough to ½ inch thickness. Cut dough to desired size and place on lightly greased baking sheet or pan with sides touching. Bake for 10–12 minutes.

Country Rolls

This modern version of an easy roll comes highly recommended from an experienced ranch cook. A good dinner roll continues to be an important staple in ranch house kitchens.

Yield: 10–12 rolls

Ingredients:
1 package active dry yeast
¼ cup sugar
1 cup warm water
2¼ cups sifted flour
1 teaspoon salt
¼ cup cooking oil

Directions:

Mix the yeast and sugar together. Add the warm water; set aside. Mix the flour and salt. Add oil to the yeast mixture; stir and pour into flour mixture. Knead several times if the dough is too sticky, but do not overwork. Form dough into a soft ball and let rise for 1 hour. Beat dough down and form rolls; place in muffin tins and let rise 45 minutes. Bake for 15–20 minutes at 400°F.

THE TRAILS

Texas longhorns were driven in all directions, not just north. To the east and near the coast, they followed the Opelousas Route, where Louisiana had shipping ports on the Red and Mississippi Rivers. Fort Sumner to the west needed beeves for the Indian reservations there and then on to California to feed gold miners and provide seed stock for establishing ranches.

Wayne Gard, president of the Texas State Historical Association, described the cattle trailing system out of Texas as a tree. The roots began in South Texas, where ranches used familiar worn paths established earlier by Native Americans and the military. At the designated gathering places, they moved northward from there toward the main route, or the trunk. Once they crossed the Red River and passed through Indian Nation, the branches offered several options to their final destination.

The easternmost route, and the earliest, was the Shawnee Trail (1846–1875). From present-day Austin, Waco, and Dallas it led into Missouri. It was the first trail to be used again after the Civil War, but the influx of homesteaders, fear of tick-caused Texas Fever, which longhorns were immune to, and the quarantines instituted by state governments that followed moved the cattle migration routes further west.

The Goodnight-Loving Trail (1866–1885), established by plainsman Charles Goodnight and his partner Oliver Loving, took a wide sweep through South Texas to avoid the Comanche hunting grounds of the Llano Estacado. He first trailed cattle to Fort Sumner in 1866 to fulfill a government contract there and advanced into Colorado. After settling a herd and establishing a ranch in Palo Duro Canyon, Goodnight blazed the Palo Duro–Dodge City Trail.

Part Cherokee and part Scottish merchant and trader, Jesse Chisholm died from food poisoning before knowing about the famous trail that bore his name. Developing contacts formed through his mother's people, he established a successful trading business with the Plains tribes. From the present site of Wichita, Kansas, Chisholm established a wagon route over which he drove supply wagons and some livestock. Chisholm actually followed parts of the same traveling route established during the Civil War by a Delaware scout named Black Beaver.

Frequently called on as an interpreter and guide, Chisholm could speak several Native American languages, and he was trusted. The Indians called him "a man with a straight tongue." He loaded wagons with manufactured goods and headed south into Indian Territory, returning with cattle, buffalo robes, and furs. At the mouth of the Little Arkansas, about ten miles north of modern-day Vernon, Texas, he built a cabin for his family. They lived in one side; in the other was his trading post.

That pesky tick and the fatal fever it caused in other cattle breeds created a panic throughout Kansas and Missouri. Cattleman Joseph McCoy moved the railhead farther west by opening stockyards at Abilene, Kansas. After crossing the Red River at Red River Station, north of present-day Fort Worth, the herds followed Chisholm's old wagon tracks to Abilene. Livestock could be taken further north to Schuyler, Nebraska, or the alternate route, which went through Ellsworth, Kansas, and on to Fort Kearny, Nebraska.

To many Texas cowmen, Chisholm's route was known simply as "the trail," or the cattle trail. "Do you wanna go up the trail?" was a common question heard often around South Texas in the early spring. Some referred to it as the Kansas Trail or the Abilene Trail. In Kansas it was known as the Texas Cattle Trail, the Wichita Trail, or the Great Cattle Trail. The point in history when it became the Chisholm Trail is unknown, but the name stuck and now refers not only to the main branch that begins in Oklahoma but also to the multiple feeder routes that existed throughout South Texas.

The Western Trail (1874–1897) ran from South Texas to Canada, the main branch being fed by numerous routes and feeder trails. The most southern tip began in Brownsville on the coast, crossing more than 700 miles to Doan's Crossing on the Red River, past Fort Supply to the first railhead at Dodge City, Kansas, and advanced further to the railhead at Ogallala, Nebraska. One route went to Fort Laramie and then to Miles City, Montana, while an alternate route went to Deadwood and Fort Buford, South Dakota. The need for beef was determined not only by the eastern markets on the Western Trail but also by the immense ranches in the north and the discovery of gold in the Black Hills. This route was the last system of trails used before the railroad extended its reach and before fencing dissected the plains.

> "The entire country east, west, and south of Salina and down to the Arkansas River is filled with Texas cattle. . . . The bottoms are overflowing with them, and the water courses with this great article of traffic. . . . And the cry is, "still they come!""
>
> SALINE COUNTY JOURNAL, JULY 20, 1871

> "We drove a herd of cattle to Alexandria, La., with W. C. Wright, who loaded them on boats for New Orleans; then we returned home."
>
> JASPER LAUDERDALE, TRAIL DRIVER

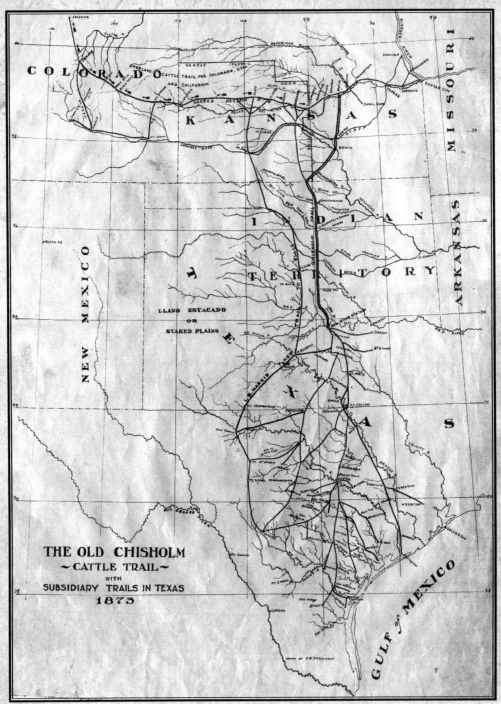

1873 Map of Chisholm Trail with subsidiary trails in Texas

Wikimedia

A long line of cattle make their way across a snowy pasture, Z/T Ranch, Pitchfork, Wyoming.
Library of Congress

"The trail to the North from Texas was started in 1867 and closed in 1895, but most of this great development was done in twenty years, from 1870 to 1890. It is conservatively estimated by old trail drivers that there were 98,000,000 cattle and 10,000,000 horse stock driven over the Northern Trails during the 28 years of trail days and that there were 35,000 men employed to handle these herds."

GEORGE W. SAUNDERS, PRESIDENT, THE OLD TIME TRAIL DRIVERS ASSOCIATION

Cowboys work in the alley of a corral sorting heifers from steers. Sanford Ranch, Texas.
Natalie Bright

CHAPTER 2
MAIN DISHES—
BEEF

In an article from the *Lola Register*, Allen County, Kansas, May 1882, a retail butcher from New York is quoted: "Everybody wants to buy prime rib roasts and porter-house and sirloin steaks, with plenty of tenderloin. You can't persuade them that the chuck roast of good beef, which is from five to eight cents a pound cheaper than the prime cut, is just as good eating."

Roasted Prime Rib of Beef

A popular dish listed in ads and on the menu of several Cowtown fine-dining establishments. Preparation is simple, and seasonings can be anything from basic salt and pepper to myriad herbs from today's cooks. Slow roasting is the key; do not overcook. Prime rib continues to be the core of a great meal more than a century later.

Yield: 1 rib per 2 people

Ingredients:

6–8 pounds ribeye roast, bone-in
Salt
½ cup butter (1 stick), softened
2 teaspoons freshly ground black pepper
2 teaspoons garlic powder

Directions:

Season beef on all sides with salt and cover loosely with plastic wrap. Allow to warm to room temperature, about 3 hours. (**Note:** Prime rib roast will cook more evenly when it's at room temperature.) Preheat oven to 500°F. Mix together spices and softened butter. Pat roast with paper towels and place bone side down in a roasting pan. Smear butter mixture on all sides. If desired, season the outside again with fresh-ground pepper. Bake at 500°F for 15 minutes, then reduce oven temperature to 325°F. Cook until done (see cooking times below). A meat thermometer is a handy tool to make sure you do not overcook your prime rib. Remove from the oven and tent with foil to rest. The roast will continue cooking while resting.

Cooking Time:

For rare, 120°F internal temperature (about 10–12 minutes per pound)

For medium rare, 125°F–130°F internal temperature (about 13–14 minutes per pound)

For medium, 130°F–140°F internal temperature (about 14–15 minutes per pound)

For medium-well or well-done, anything over 140°F, all of the fat will melt out of the meat, leaving it tough, dry. and the consistency of a boot.

Pot Roast and Sour Cream Gravy

Dated 1891 and credited to a hotel in Denver, Colorado, this reminds me of a variation of beef Stroganoff that uses a roast instead of steak.

Yield: About 8 servings

Ingredients:

1 (4-pound) beef pot roast

3 tablespoons cooking fat

1 beef bouillon cube

1 cup boiling water

4 tablespoons catsup

1 tablespoon Worcestershire sauce

1 tablespoon minced onion

½ clove garlic, minced

2 teaspoons salt

1 teaspoon celery seed

½ teaspoon black pepper

4 tablespoons flour

1 small can mushrooms

1 cup dairy sour cream

Directions:

Brown pot roast in fat in a Dutch oven or kettle. Pour off drippings. Dissolve bouillon cube in the boiling water; add to roast. Add catsup, Worcestershire, onion, garlic, salt, celery seed, and pepper. Cover and cook over low fire (250°F) for 2½–3 hours, or until meat is tender. Remove meat from Dutch oven or kettle. Blend flour and mushroom liquid (reserve mushrooms), and stir into remaining beef liquid to make gravy. Add mushrooms. Remove kettle from fire and stir in sour cream. Serve slices of pot roast with gravy.

"This trip marked by excessive rainfall, big rains falling at night, and one hailstorm, adding greatly to the hardship of the cowboy's lot; but we didn't mind it much and, with songs and jokes, kept up our spirits."

G. W. MILLS, TRAIL DRIVER

Cheyenne Steak

A steak dish credited to a hotel in Cheyenne, Wyoming, that features a somewhat dated method to prepare beefsteak, but the basic idea is still used today.

Yield: 4–6 servings

Ingredients:

3 pounds sirloin steak, cut 2 inches thick
1 tablespoon black peppercorns
2 cloves garlic, minced
4 cups coarse salt
¾ cup water

Directions:

Trim excess fat from steak. Crack peppercorns coarsely, and mince garlic. Press peppercorns and garlic into both sides of steak and let stand at room temperature for 1 hour. Make a thick paste of salt and water; cover top side of peppered steak with one-half the mixture. If cooking steak over coals, cover salt side with a wet cloth and place salt side down on grill. (Cloth or paper holds the salt in place; it will char as the steak cooks, but this does not affect the taste.) Cover top side with remaining salt mixture and another piece of wet cloth. If broiling, leave the cloth off and put salt side up, 3 inches from broiler heat. Put salt on the other side of the steak when it is turned. Cook 15 minutes on each side for rare, 25 minutes for medium rare. Remove salt before eating.

"We would often ride through the streets of Tascosa, apply the spurs just right and put on a bronc show for the folks."

TOM COFFEE, TRAIL DRIVER

Simple Hash

Hash is an easy use of leftovers, first appearing in the United States around 1860. Versions of hash can be traced all over the world with the same basic ingredients of beef or corned beef, potatoes, and onions. Hash can be served for breakfast, lunch or dinner.

Yield: 4–5 servings

Ingredients:

4 cups cooked beef, ground or chopped (leftover)

2 cups chopped, cooked potatoes (leftover)

1 cup chopped onion

1 teaspoon salt

¼ teaspoon pepper

¼ teaspoon sage

½ cup meat juice or leftover gravy

¼ cup bacon fat or lard

Directions:

Mix meat, potatoes, onions, and seasonings; moisten with meat juice. Heat bacon fat in heavy skillet. Add hash mixture and fry slowly until brown and crisp.

"Two days after we struck camp southwest of Dodge City, several of the cowboys were excused by the boss to go to town for supplies. Soon after they arrived there they began to 'tank up' on mean whiskey and proceeded to shoot up the town. As they came out at a high rate of speed, one of them, John Briley, was killed by the marshal of Dodge City. I was in Dodge City the next day and saw that he was buried. Associating with bad company has cost many a man his life."

T. J. BRUKETT, TRAIL DRIVER

BAT MASTERSON AND THE PRAIRIE DOG

Born in Quebec, Bartholemew William Barclay Masterson, known as "Bat," moved with his family to Kansas. Leaving home at age seventeen, he became a memorable character of the Western frontier, making his living first as a buffalo hunter and then a US Army scout and professional gambler. His reputation as a gunman emerged during a shootout in Mobeetie, Texas, where he worked as a young faro dealer. Bat and an army sergeant tangled over a dance-hall girl named Mollie Brennan. Bat was the only survivor but occasionally relied on a walking cane the rest of his life.

Fleeing Texas, Bat followed the gold strike to South Dakota and reportedly showed up in other places north. While playing at the gaming tables in Cheyenne, Wyatt Earp encouraged him to consider the new fledgling Cowtowns. Soon after settling in Dodge City, Bat won the election as Ford County sheriff by three votes, and repeated legends solidified his reputation as a brave and hard man. He eventually left frontier life behind and, while living in Denver, Colorado, took an interest in prizefighting, dealt faro, and married singer and juggler Emma Moulton. The couple moved to New York City, where Bat lived the life of a newspaperman, writing a sports column for the *Morning Telegraph*. His name continues to be connected to the Wild West's most iconic events, and his favorite sandwich lives on in Cowtown lore.

Old Mobeetie Cemetery, Texas Panhandle
Natalie Bright

The Prairie Dog

This flavorful hot dog is credited to Bat Masterson during his time as a lawman in Cowtown. Featuring a unique addition of sage on the meat plus mustard and Worcestershire sauce on the bun, the sandwich became popular throughout the Old West.

Yield: 2 servings

Ingredients:

2 hot dog wieners
2 buns
Ground sage
Mustard
Dill pickles, thinly sliced
Worcestershire sauce

Directions:

Split each wiener lengthwise. Generously rub inside the slit with the ground sage. Broil until brown. Spread one side of the bun with mustard and cover with the thinly sliced dill pickles. Sprinkle the other side of the bun with Worcestershire sauce. Add the cooked wiener and enjoy.

Famed lawman turned newspaper man Bat Masterson
Library of Congress

Mustard Short Ribs

The tangy taste of mustard tingles your tongue—a unique substitute for the standard barbecue sauce.

Yield: 6–8 servings

Ingredients:

4 pounds beef short ribs, cut into pieces

⅓ cup prepared mustard

1 tablespoon white wine or lemon juice

2 cloves garlic, crushed

1 tablespoon sugar

1 teaspoon salt

½ teaspoon pepper

4 medium onions, sliced

¼ cup shortening

Directions:

Place meat in a shallow glass dish. Mix mustard, wine or lemon juice, garlic, sugar, salt, and pepper; spread on meat. Top with onions. Cover tightly and refrigerate for 24 hours, turning meat occasionally. The next day, in a preheated Dutch oven, brown ribs in shortening over medium heat; pour off drippings. Add onions and pour leftover marinade over meat. Cover tightly; cook in 350°F oven for 2 hours.

"I started preparations with seven Mexicans, about 30 horses, and a packhorse. The Mexicans could not speak English and I could not speak Spanish. I did not know any of the range and thought I was up against a hard proposition but, believe me, we brought home the goods."

W. T. (BILL) JACKMAN, TRAIL DRIVER

Meat and Gravy Casserole

Try this unique combination of ingredients with beef, bison, or pork.

Yield: 6–8 servings

Ingredients:

6 tablespoons butter

¼ pound onions, sliced

½ pound green sour apples, sliced

¾ pound cooked beef, pork, or bison

2½ pounds potatoes, sliced and cooked

Salt to taste

Pepper to taste

Nutmeg, to taste

2½ cups meat gravy or stock

½ cup buttered breadcrumbs

"At Dodge City every man, including the boss, except myself, celebrated in great style, while I was left to handle and hold the outfit."

GEORGE W. BROCK,
TRAIL DRIVER

Directions:

Preheat oven to 350°F. Melt 3 tablespoons butter in a heavy skillet and add onions; sauté until golden brown. Remove the rings. Melt remaining butter and sauté the apple slices. In a small casserole dish, layer a portion of the potatoes, meat, onions, and apples. Season with salt, pepper, and nutmeg. Repeat layers until all are used. Cover with meat stock or gravy. Top with buttered breadcrumbs and bake at 350°F for 1 hour.

A barroom in Detroit. Cowtown developers spared no expense
to mimic the fine dining establishments of the East.
Library of Congress

Cookstove Meat Loaf

Credited to the cook at the TZ Ranch, Globe, Arizona.

Yield: 6–8 servings

Ingredients:

1 pound ground beef
¼ pound pork sausage
1 egg, beaten
1 tablespoon butter, crumbled
2 slices bread, crumbled
1 onion, finely chopped
1 teaspoon salt
⅛ teaspoon black pepper
¼ teaspoon ground sage
1 beef bouillon cube
½ cup boiling water
4 strips raw bacon
4 tablespoons chili sauce

Directions:

Preheat oven to 350°F. Combine all ingredients except last four. Dissolve bouillon in the boiling water and add to mixture. Shape into a loaf and place in greased baking pan. Top with bacon strips. After meat has baked about 25 minutes, spread chili sauce over the top and return to oven for remaining time. Total baking time: 45–50 minutes.

"Take the cowboy; to be sure he did lots of raw things but he lived in the rawest of surroundings."

CHARLIE COWBOY

Nellie's Cabbage and Beef Buns

Credited to Nellie's Rooming House, a brothel in Abilene, Kansas. Some brothels offered hot meals to their customers in addition to alcohol and entertainment.

Yield: About 24 meat-filled buns

Ingredients:
3 pounds ground beef
2 heads cabbage, chopped
2 onions, chopped
Salt and pepper, to taste
Bread or sweet-roll dough
Melted butter

Directions:

Break meat into small pieces in a large heavy skillet. Simmer meat in its own juices for 20–25 minutes, stirring often until done. Cook cabbage and onions together until cabbage has wilted down. Drain off all liquid from cabbage and meat, and then mix together. Add salt and pepper, to taste. Using regular bread or sweet-roll dough, roll out dough on floured board to ¼ inch thick. Cut into squares about 6 x 6 inches. Place about 3 tablespoons of meat filling in center of each square; lift up corners and pinch edges. When sealed, pat out gently to pull out corners. Place seam side down on greased pan, and brush top with melted butter. Let rise 20–25 minutes; then bake at 325°F for 25 minutes, or until golden brown. Serve hot.

"You can't read a cow's mind eatin' chicken."

JOE SURSA, NEW MEXICO RANCH FOREMAN

DOAN'S CROSSING

Corwin Doan moved to a popular herd crossing on the Red River near the Western Trail, ten miles north of Vernon, Texas, to work with his Uncle Jonathon and establish a trading post there.

Doan knew many of the great Native American chiefs during that time, such as Big Bow, chief of the Kiowas, and the famous Comanche chief Quanah Parker. Chief Quanah left Texas to position himself in the Wichita Mountains near Fort Sill, where he exacted a beef toll from each trail herd he confronted. Doan often gave away crackers and candy to the Indian women and children when they traveled to the trading post.

It was Kiowa chief Satanta who warned Doan to leave because some of the Indians liked him and they were planning raids in the area with the intention of killing every White man in the Nation. One evening at dusk, he returned home after hunting to learn that Indians on horses had been sighted. Taking the women, a baby, and a dog, they spent the night in a grove of trees located about a half mile from his house.

Doan recalled: "The Kiowas told me afterward quite coolly that they would have attacked us that night but believed us to be heavily garrisoned with buffalo hunters—a lucky thing for us. This was the last raid through the country. The Indians after that became very friendly with us and told me to go ahead and build a big store; that we would not be molested. They had decided this in council."

Doan's daughter, Bertha Doan Ross, grew up knowing most of the leading cattlemen of the day as well as the great Indian chiefs. In an interview for the *Wichita Falls Times*, she remembered that Quanah Parker and his Comanche braves spent much time at the Doan store. "He was a rascal," she said and admitted that he was a credit to both the White race and the Indians.

> "My first introduction to the Old Chisholm Trail was in 1874 when in company with Robert E. Doan, a cousin, and both of us from Wilmington, Ohio, we set out for Ft. Sill, Indian Territory, from Wichita, Kansas. We made this little jaunt by stagecoach of 250 miles over the famous trail in good time."
>
> C. F. DOAN, DOAN'S STORE

> "The first house at Doan's was made of pickets with a dirt roof and floor of the same material. The first winter we had no door, but a buffalo robe did service against the northers. The store which had consisted mainly of ammunition and a few groceries occupied one end and the family lived in the other."
>
> CORWIN F. DOAN OF DOAN'S CROSSING

Satanta (White Bear), Kiowa chief
Library of Congress

It was the spring and summer of 1879 when Doan remembers witnessing the first of the herds that came up the trail. "One hundred thousand cattle passed over the trail by the little store in 1879. In 1881 the trail reached the peak of production and three hundred and one thousand were driven by to the Kansas shipping point."

Doan's Store became an important supply station, stocking provisions for cowboys, buffalo hunters, settlers, and the Native American tribes of the area. It was the last stop before crossing the vast plains of the Indian Nation. Supplies arrived from Denison, Sherman, and Gainesville. The store did a thriving business, selling everything you could imagine: cartridges, Winchesters by the case, sowbelly, flour, and even Stetson hats. By 1880 the community consisted of the store, a hotel, a saloon, and a school, growing to a population of around 200 people. Doan kept copious records, but unfortunately his journals were destroyed. History records' best estimates are that six million head of Texas longhorns and one million horses forded the Red River at Doan's Crossing.

Doan's monument
Panhandle-Plains Historical Museum, Canyon, Texas

During that first year, Corwin Doan was declared postmaster, and the US Post Office Department designated his store as a post office. Thereafter, all mail for the trail herds was routed through that location. "Many a sweetheart down the trail received her letter bearing the postmark of Doan's, and many a cowboy asked self-consciously if there was any mail for him while his face turned a beet red when a dainty missive was handed him," Doan wrote.

The tradition of the Doan's picnic began in 1884 with five women and one man and has since grown to thousands in attendance. It is still held at the adobe house that remains on the site. A monument was erected in memory of the trail drivers in 1931.

"In 1881 our present home was built, the year the county was organized. This dwelling I still occupy. Governors, English Lords, bankers, lawyers, tramps, and people from every walk of life have found sanctuary within its walls."

C. F. DOAN

SUNDAY DINNER AT THE PACIFIC HOTEL

Union Pacific Hotel and Depot, Abilene, Kansas

ɹ

SUNDAY DINNER

ɹ

An Attractive Menu Arranged by the Pacific Hotel.

The menu for the Union Pacific hotel's Sunday dinner
tomorrow is given below.
Only 25 cents to residents of the city.

MENU.

ɹ

Clam Chowder
Boil Trout, Natural Sauce
Potatoes au gratin
Lettuce. Olives. Sliced Cucumbers. Sliced Tomatoes.
Boiled Sugar Cured Ham
Roast Sirloin of Beef
Ribs of Beef, browned potatoes
Roast Turkey, Sage dressing
Smothered Chicken, Southern Style
White Cake, lemon sauce
Mashed Potatoes. Green Peas.
New Boiled Potatoes. Wax Beans.
Pickled Beets. Salmon Salad.
Strawberry Short Cake.
Apple Pie. Lemon Pie.
Vanilla Ice Cream.
Cream Cheese. Assorted Cake.
Assorted Fruit. Raisins. Assorted Nuts.
Coffee. Ice Tea. Sweet Milk.

Abilene Daily Reflector, June 1894

Cattle buyer at Denver, Colorado, stockyards
Library of Congress

CHAPTER 3

MAIN DISHES— PORK AND FISH

Stockyard Ham

This unique recipe is credited to two different stockyard restaurants, one in Victoria, Texas, and another in Arizona. Claimed to be the "best ham you can cook," you have to start with a first-quality, uncooked ham. I can imagine how the best recipes made their way across the West to be shared and prepared by other establishments.

Yield: 12–15 servings

Ingredients
11- to14-pound ham, bone-in
1 cup sugar per 1 quart water
Whole cloves, enough to cover ham
3 tablespoons brown sugar
1 tablespoon flour
1 quart dry red or white wine
2 cups reserved sugar-syrup water
2 tablespoons flour
¼ cup cold water

Directions:

Be sure to purchase a quality uncured ham. Remove the skin with a sharp knife so that the meat will absorb the syrup. In a large kettle or Dutch oven, cover the ham with the cold water and sugar mixture, using 1 cup sugar to every quart of water. Stir until sugar is dissolved. Slowly bring to a boil, which takes about 1 hour, and boil for 10 minutes. Turn off heat and remove pot from stove. Let ham soak and cool in the syrup for about 24 hours. After soak, return to stovetop and bring it to a second boil. Reduce heat and simmer for 12 minutes per pound of ham. (An 11-pound ham would need to simmer for about 2 hours.) Remove ham from syrup mixture, reserving sugar-syrup water, and place ham in a roasting pan. Stick cloves over entire ham, 1½ inches apart. Mix brown sugar and flour together. Cover the top side of ham with a ½-inch-thick layer of brown sugar mixture. Add 1 quart of wine and 2 cups of the reserved sugar syrup. Roast in a slow oven (300°F) for 45 minutes, basting ham with wine mixture every 10 minutes.

Special Ham Sauce

Directions:

In a saucepan, add 2 cups sugar-syrup liquid left over from the roasted ham; skim grease off the top. To every 2 cups liquid add 1 cup wine and 1 teaspoon prepared mustard; stir until well dissolved. Bring to a boil. To thicken, mix 2 tablespoons flour with ¼ cup cold water. Mix well then stir into sauce. Cook to proper consistency; remove from heat. Strain and serve with ham.

BUSINESS TOWN

The necessary players involved in the cattle trade included a varied mix of occupations. The landowner or rancher who raised the cattle was not usually directly involved in moving them to market. A trailing contractor guaranteed delivery of the herd to the railhead in Cowtown, charging a delivery fee of $1.00 to $1.50 per head. He furnished all supplies and wagons, hired drovers, and found capable trail bosses who knew the route. This relieved the burden of organizing a drive for smaller ranch owners.

A herd of 3,000 cows could be driven relatively cheaply: eleven drovers at $30/month; one cook at $50/month; one trail boss at $100/month; provisions, $100+ for a three- to four-month trip at a direct expense outlay of less than $1,000. With cattle selling anywhere from $20 to as much as $80 per head, that's a nice profit.

Many successful ranchers built their enterprises in this way—buying livestock, driving them to Cowtown railheads, and selling them for hefty profits to the packing house representatives.

At the end of the trail, the stockyard promoter worked with city councils and railroad representatives, and the meat packer maintained the continuous supply for their bosses back East. The railroads charge a per-head fee for transportation, anywhere from $2.50 per head and up. In some instances it was cheaper to drive them to alternate railheads. For example, Dallas to St. Louis, the charge could be around $5.50 per head, whereas the Santa Fe Line out of Ellsworth charged only $3.50 per head.

Opened in 1871 to offer livestock owners better prices than the railroads, the Kansas City Stockyards became the second largest, handling 170,000 animals per day.
Library of Congress

The Stockyards in Denver, Colorado, opened in 1886 with pens and elevated
viewing walkways, eventually covering 105 acres.
Library of Congress

The commission merchant between sellers and buyers purchased trail
livestock on speculation to be fattened up and sold later to meat packers or
to ranchers looking to build their herds. Bankers slid into the mix as well.
Banks issued credit to trail bosses to pay the drovers, replenish supplies for
extended drives, and pay expenses while living in Cowtown until a suitable
deal could be made with a buyer. Abilene Mayor Joseph McCoy referred cattlemen to the First National Bank of Kansas City, where a reported $900,000
had passed through that bank in its first two months of operation.

City newspapers kept citizens updated on market activity of the day. The
Dodge City Times of July 17, 1880, reports, "Seventy-five thousand head of
cattle are being driven from Colorado to the range in Western Kansas. Four
cars of beef were shipped from this point to Colorado this week."

Another article in the same edition of the *Dodge City Times* reports on
the weather conditions and assures the townspeople of a successful season:
"Cattle are selling at very good prices. The drought in Colorado has been a
serious drawback, as that state is a good market for Texas stock. The location of new cattle ranchers in this section will tend to create a larger market. The increase in the cattle trade will add largely to the business of this
city and will insure a traffic summer and winter."

The Great Union Stockyards, Chicago, grew to employ 40,000 people by 1921 and established Chicago as the meat processing center of the world.
Cattle Raisers Museum, Fort Worth, Texas

A piece in the *Kansas Cowboy* out of Dodge City (1884), assured its readers of the importance of the town. "Dodge is a lively business town. The amount of freight received here over the Atchinson, Topeka and Santa Fe Railway is enormous, as this is the base of supplies for the immense country of which this the centre. It is also a government distribution post."

"In those early days, cattle buyers usually met the sellers at some appointed place to close a deal for stock, and they would bring the purchase money in gold and silver in sacks on the backs of packhorses. When they reached the meeting places the sacks of money would be carelessly dumped on the ground, where sometimes it would remain for two or three days without molestation, then when the settlement was made for cattle bought, the sacks were opened, the money dumped out on a blanket in camp, and counted out to each man who had participated in the trades. I fear that kind of an arrangement would not work today, but in those days those rugged pioneers dealt strictly on the square."

GEORGE W. SAUNDERS, TRAIL DRIVER

Glazed Pork Ribs

Always a classic favorite, but this modern version is simple and flavorful.

Yield: 6–8 servings

Ingredients:

4 pounds spareribs

1 (15-ounce) can tomato sauce

1 (7-ounce) envelope onion soup and dip mix

¼ cup vinegar

¼ cup light molasses

2 tablespoons salad oil

2 teaspoons dry mustard

1 cup water

Directions:

Place spareribs meaty side up in a shallow roasting pan. Heat remaining ingredients to boiling, stirring constantly. Boil and stir 3 minutes. Pour sauce over meat. Roast in 350°F oven for 1½ hours or until done, basting 4–5 times while cooking.

"The range was full of wild mustang horses, and they caused us a lot of trouble, for we had to keep our horse stock from getting with them, for once they got mixed with the mustangs they soon became as wild or wilder than these wild horses."

GEORGE W. SAUNDERS, TRAIL DRIVER

Double D Pork Roast

Credited to the cook, who worked at a ranch in Iowa.

Yield: 6–8 servings

Ingredients:

3- to 5-pound pork roast

3 bay leaves, crumbled

3 cloves garlic, minced

½ teaspoon thyme

1¾ tablespoons chopped parsley

2 tablespoons paprika

½ teaspoon salt

3½ tablespoons minced onion

Juice of 1 lemon

⅓ cup white wine

Directions:

Score fat on pork roast and place in roasting pan. Combine the next 7 ingredients; mix and rub over the skin of the pork. Roast meat in 350°F oven for 30 minutes. Remove fat from bottom of pan. Combine lemon juice and wine. Continue to roast the pork for 1½ hours, basting with wine mixture. Add additional liquid to pan if necessary.

"I went to Dodge City, the honkatonk town, cleaned up and bought a suit of clothes, and left for San Antonio, reaching home July 1, 1885."

JOHN B. CONNER, TRAIL DRIVER

Turnips and Pork

"Sweet Water Shorty" cooked on a ranch in Utah and served several pork dishes to the working cowboys that passed through.

Yield: 8–12 servings

Ingredients:

3 pounds pork loin

3 pounds turnips, sliced

1½ pounds potatoes, sliced

1 teaspoon salt

1 tablespoon sugar

Black pepper, to taste

Directions:

Boil pork loin in salted water to cover until well done (several hours). Remove pork to baking pan; brown in a preheated 350°F oven for 35 minutes. Remove pork and set aside. Place turnips and potatoes in alternate layers in pork juice. Add salt, sugar, and pepper to taste. Cook until tender. Serve with pork.

"There must have been eight or ten large outfits camped within only five miles of each other; it was quite a sight."

JIM LESSER, TRAIL DRIVER

THE MOST BEAUTIFUL WOMAN IN DODGE

The Union Pacific Railroad advanced their line, causing Ellsworth to lose out to another Cowtown, soon to be known as the "wickedest little city in America" and the "Babylon of the plains."

Its name was Dodge City.

On the Santa Fe Trail and five miles west of Fort Dodge, H. L. Sitler constructed a sod house in 1871. Within one year the site had a general store, three dance halls, and six saloons. The Santa Fe Railroad reached Dodge City in 1872. Texas cattle drovers took an alternate route, diverting from the main Chisholm Trail to Dodge City, establishing a new route referred to as the Texas Trail. Thousands of longhorn cattle were driven over the Texas Trail into Dodge City and loaded onto the railcars. As with the other Cowtowns, Dodge City leaders advertised and vied for the trail bosses, promising top-notch food and accommodations and first-class entertainment for their trail hands.

Newspapers fondly remember one singer in particular. In addition to a mesmerizing voice and striking beauty, Dora Hand had a reputation for having a giving spirit and being an exceptional cook. Performing under the stage name of Fannie Keenan, she sang nightly at the Lady Gay Theatre for the cattle trailing crowds and every Sunday at church, which gained her fans from the town's respectable citizens as well. Unfortunately, she came to a violent end at the age of only thirty-four.

"The Killing of Dora Hand" was the shocking headline in the *Dodge City Times*, October 1878. On that ill-fated night, Dora and her friend Fannie Garretson stayed at the small shack of Mayor Dog Kelley while he was out of town for a medical procedure. Early morning, around 4:00 a.m., a cowboy on a horse rode into the yard and fired shots into the mayor's home. Tragically, one shot passed through the first room, through the plaster partition, and struck Dora Hand in the right side. She died instantly. Texas cowboy and troublemaker Spike Kenedy was blamed because he had it in for Kelley. The mayor had thrown Spike out of the bar he owned. Some versions claim that their feud began over the attention Spike paid to the beautiful entertainer because she and Mayor Kelley were engaged to be married, but some accounts refute that theory.

Ford County Sheriff Bat Masterson formed a posse, which included Marshal Charlie Basset, Wyatt Earp, and Bill Tilghman. They presumed that Kenedy would head south, back to Texas, and decided to cut him off.

Dora Hand
Wikimedia

Despite a stormy night, they succeeded. The murderer's capture the next day resulted in his getting shot in the left shoulder. Spike asked if the mayor was dead. Upon hearing the news that he had killed Dora instead, Spike raged at Bat Masterson: "You ought to have made a better shot than you did!"

Texas rancher Mifflin Kenedy, cofounder of the famed King Ranch in South Texas, arrived in Dodge City and to his injured son's aid. Spike's trial was held and he was released, as there were no witnesses who had actually seen him pull the trigger. Was it the lack of evidence or the rumored $25,000 fee paid by his father?

The claim was made that Dora had moved out West because of tuberculosis, leaving behind a wealthy Boston family and a career as an opera singer. Or perhaps it was to escape an unhappy marriage to musician Theodore Hand. Regardless as to the why, the drovers had welcomed her with enthusiasm. The *Dodge City Times* reported that "her artful and winning ways brought many admirers within her smiles and blandishments." The charming and graceful Dora Hand was laid to rest with the most elaborate funeral ever witnessed; more than 400 mounted cowboys lined the streets of Dodge City as her coffin passed.

Sandwich Dora Hand

The fish sandwich that bears the name of this beloved Cowtown performer became a legendary Dodge City favorite.

Yield: 1 sandwich

Ingredients:
6–8 ounces fresh fish per person, cleaned
2 tablespoons vinegar
¼ teaspoon black pepper
½ teaspoon salt
2 slices bread or 1 hamburger bun
4 tablespoons butter, softened
Dill pickles, sliced
Onion, thinly sliced
Mustard

Directions:

Fill a pot with water. Add vinegar, pepper, and salt. Boil fish until done, about 3–9 minutes. Remove fish, drain on paper toweling, and debone. Set aside. Butter both slices of bread with 2 tablespoons of the butter. Melt the remaining 2 tablespoons butter in a heated cast-iron skillet over medium heat. Add the fish. Chunk and mash up fish as it cooks, stirring continuously until lightly browned. Spread a thick layer of fish on one piece of bread. Top with thinly sliced dill pickles and then the onion. Top that with mustard. Cover with the top bun and serve warm.

THE PEACEKEEPERS

The wild stories of lawlessness and wickedness are many, enhanced in the telling because those Lone Star boys always stuck together when trouble happened. In an effort to keep control, various ordinances were passed.

City leaders relocated the more sinful areas away from the respectable citizens, where the undesirables could be cornered off in their own section of Cowtown. Fun could be had one-half mile east of Ellsworth in a place called Nauch-ville, or "the bottom," where, among other things, horse races were

Wild Bill Hickok, Texas Jack Omohundro, and Buffalo Bill Cody
Wikimedia

No sheriff west of Newton—no God west of Dodge.

held. In Newton, "Hide Park" lay on the south side of the railroad tracks. The area on the east edge of Abilene where the brothels and gambling houses were located was called "McCoy's Addition," after Joseph McCoy, the man who brought the cattle trade to the little settlement.

In Wichita, "horse-thief corner" was located east of the Texas House saloon, where horse auctions were held regularly. The tough district was called Delano, where the impeccably dressed couple, Rowdy Joe Lowe and his wife, Kate, ran "the swiftest joint in Kansas." Arrests were made and fines were collected, for a total of $5,600 in one cattle season, which paid salaries of the law enforcement to police the city. Wichita's city marshal made $91.60 per month; the assistant marshal, $75; and the deputies, $60 a month.

City ordinances were passed to appease concerned citizens. The imposed fines were collected once a year, and then it was business as usual. Some towns required all visitors to leave their weapons at a collection place, and city leaders employed men with tough reputations to uphold the law.

City marshals were hired by the mayor and town councils. Along with their deputies, they acted as peace officers within the city limits. At the county level, sheriffs were usually the highest elected official within the county government and also had a group of deputies under their control. They collected taxes on a countywide basis.

Federal or deputy US marshals investigated crimes within a specified region. They might also hold the position of town marshal or county sheriff. Wyatt Earp served as a deputy officer in both Wichita and Dodge City. He served both as a federal deputy marshal and as an appointed deputy in Tombstone, Arizona. His brother Virgil was Tombstone city marshal and a deputy US marshal.

Wild Bill Hickok was hired to be the marshal of Abilene, Kansas. Known as a two-gun man, he could draw both revolvers fast and shoot with deadly accuracy. Among other tricks, he could toss a spinning hat in the air and shoot the brim full of holes. That kind of reputation made rowdy drovers

Posted at the four main highways leading into Wichita, Kansas:
EVERYTHING GOES IN WICHITA
Leave your Revolvers at Police
Headquarters and get a Check.
CARRYING CONCEALED WEAPONS
STRICTLY FORBIDDEN

think twice before starting any trouble. His salary was $150 per month plus one-quarter of all money collected in fines. Shucking his buckskins for a Prince Albert jacket, checkered trousers, and embroidered silk vest, this handsome man who stood over six feet tall must have made an impressive lawman. He set up his office in the Alamo Saloon, a popular, ornately decorated place with glass doors that remained open to the street. Instead of making rounds like his predecessor, Hickok gambled most days and nights as a way to supplement his salary.

In Newton, law enforcement was funded by a $150 county license fee paid by saloon owners. They also collected a gambling tribute, which allowed the professional gamblers to run games in the saloons. By August 1871, Newton had twenty-seven places where liquor was sold and eight gambling houses.

Wild Bill Hickok
Wikimedia

Despite the continued reputation of lawlessness and uncontrolled wickedness, Robert Dykstra compiled homicide statistics from Cowtown newspapers. Over a period from 1870 to 1885, he records a total of forty-five homicides, which involved the cities of Abilene, Ellsworth, Wichita, Dodge City, and Caldwell. The majority of deaths were identified as officers of the law, cowboys, or gamblers.

There were some who had fond memories of their time living in Cowtown. Vaudeville comedian Eddie Foy spent two summers in Dodge City. In his memoir he noted, "I can testify, however, that the majority of days passed rather peacefully in Dodge, with no killings and few fights."

Mexican cowboy eating dinner after the roundup (cattle ranch near Marfa, Texas)
Library of Congress

CHAPTER 4

SOUPS, STEWS, AND SIDES

"On a plain about halfway between the Red Fork and the Salt Fork we had to stop our herds until the buffalo passed. Buffalo, horses, elk, deer, antelope, wolves, and some cattle were all mixed together, and it took several hours for them to pass, with our assistance, so that we could proceed on our journey. I think there were more buffalo in that herd than I ever saw of any living thing, unless it was an army of grasshoppers in Kansas in July 1874."

B. A. BORROUM, TRAIL DRIVER

Utah Kelly's 7-Bean Soup

Credited to the famed cook at the 4-Bar T Ranch in Salt Lake City, Utah.

Yield: 8–10 servings

Ingredients:

8 cups water

1 pound dried beans, 7 kinds (your choice)

2 cups ham chunks or ham hocks

1 tablespoon lard or bacon grease

½ teaspoon salt

½ teaspoon black pepper

½ cup chopped onions

½ cup chopped tomatoes

½ stalk celery

½ cup bell pepper

Directions:

Sort and rinse beans; let soak in warm water for 1½ hours. Discard water, and cover beans with fresh water. Cook on medium heat for 1½ hours. While beans are cooking, cook ham in bacon grease with seasonings and vegetables (as desired). Add to beans and cook until beans are tender, 45 minutes–2 hours, depending on variety. Serve with corn bread. For leftovers, reheat and add cooked rice.

Cowmen were producing cattle long before the trails headed north.
Natalie Bright

Arizona Pot Stew

This 1886-dated recipe is credited to the Steerhead Saloon in Show Low, Arizona, a real town with an interesting story behind the name. Realizing they could not work together, two ranch owners decided to settle the matter over poker in 1876. With no clear winner after the marathon card game, they agreed to a "show-of-low" in order to declare the winner of it all.

Yield: 6–8 servings

Ingredients:
1½ pounds lean stew beef
1 pint water
Salt, to taste
1 onion, sliced
Pepper, to taste
3 tablespoons sugar
2 teaspoons cinnamon
1 pint tomato juice or crushed tomatoes

Directions:

Combine stew beef, water, and salt. Cook slowly until tender, letting the water decrease to about 1 cup. Add remaining ingredients and continue cooking over low heat, stirring occasionally to keep from sticking, until the red gravy begins to thicken. Cinnamon and sugar may be adjusted to taste. Serve over mashed potatoes.

"There were some fifty herds of Longhorns grazing along the Arkansas River outside of Dodge City when a thunderstorm struck. It was a week before the herds were back in place."

JIM HUNTER, TRAIL DRIVER

Poor Cowboy's Stew

A combination of beef and chicken makes a hearty dish.

Yield: 10–12 servings

Ingredients:

4 pounds chuck steak, cubed

2 pounds chicken, shredded

6 cups water

2 teaspoons salt

Pepper, to taste

5 slices bacon

1 quart tomatoes

½ cup chopped onion

1 cup cubed carrots

½ cup chopped celery

1 cup cubed potatoes

½ cup chopped green pepper

¼ teaspoon crushed red pepper

½ clove garlic, minced

2 cloves

1 bay leaf

3 ears corn (about 2 cups)

1 pint butter beans

½ cup flour

parsley for garnish

Directions:

Combine meat, water, salt, and pepper; cook until meat is tender. Fry bacon, retaining grease; crumble. Add tomatoes, onions, carrots, celery, potatoes, green pepper, crushed red pepper, garlic, cloves, and bay leaf. Simmer at least 1 hour. Remove bay leaf and cloves. Add corn from the cob and undrained beans; simmer 30 minutes. Blend flour and bacon grease; add to pot and simmer, stirring until the liquid thickens. Add more salt if needed. Garnish with parsley and crumbled bacon.

Nobody but cattle know why they stampede, and they ain't talking.

LET'S
ENTERTAIN
THEM

Rivalry between the Kansas Cowtowns grew fierce, and the business of enticing the ranch owners and their trail bosses back year after year took on a serious nature. Towns invested heavily in these ventures by constructing ornate establishments. Local newspaper editors stood behind their cities by touting the merits of their community while reporting on the disputes and dangers of neighboring towns.

City councils worked to entice the best in entertainment, orchestras, dramatic companies, and vocalists. Saloons advertised high-stakes gambling and the most beautiful girls; motels bragged about the finest in dining and accommodations. Ensuring a base of repeat customers became a yearlong effort. Some towns took things a step further. Ellsworth built a racetrack

Dodge City Cow-Boy Band
Library of Congress

for horse racing. Wichita boasted about having a racetrack too—and about having the most "soiled doves." Outfitted in leather leggings, red bandanas, six-shooters, and spurs, the Dodge City Cow-Boy Band performed nightly in front of the Long Branch Saloon.

Dodge City hosted horse and dog races and contracted for the construction of the Varieties Theatre. The contract stipulated that the job be finished in ten days, but it opened in eight. The *Dodge City Times* reported that the Varieties "presented the extravagant Can-Can to large and appreciative audiences"—a first for Cowtown. The scandalous, high-energy dance revealed ankles and other "specialties" because of the performers' high kicks and cartwheels.

Vaudeville comedian Eddie Foy recalls his arrival in Dodge City in his book *Clowning Through Life*: "One of the most vivid of my first impressions of Dodge yet remaining is that of dust; heat, wind, and flat prairie, too, but above all dust." Along with his stage partner, Jim Thompson, Foy arrived on the Santa Fe line. "There was just one train a day into Dodge from the East, and the whole town turned out to meet it. . . . Thompson and I were engaged to work at the combined concert and dance hall and gambling house owned by a man named Ben Springer, and as we were a star attraction direct from Chicago, Ben met us at the train."

Eddie Foy
Wikimedia

Springer introduced the performers to the town officials. Foy recalls meeting one man who made an impression. "Almost the first person to whom he presented me was a trim, good-looking young man with a pleasant face and carefully barbered mustache, well-tailored clothes, hat with a rakish tilt and two big Silver-mounted, ivory-handled pistols in a heavy belt. 'This is our sheriff, Mr. Masterson,' said Springer. 'Bat, we call him.' Masterson and I soon took a liking to each other, and were friends thenceforward."

Merchant and former mayor of Dodge City Alonzo Webster took the notion of entertaining the summer guests in an even more distinctive way. They needed a big event to be held on the July 4, 1884, holiday, and Webster had a brilliant idea. Dodge City would host the first ever authentic bullfight!

> "The audacity of the town is wonderful.... Where is there
> another town in the country that would have the nerve to
> get up a genuine Spanish bull fight on American soil?"
>
> *KANSAS COWBOY* NEWSPAPER, 1884

Webster organized the Driving Park and Fair Association and raised
$10,000 from city merchants and business leaders to build an arena, chutes,
and a grandstand. The association wanted to hire "genuine Spanish bullfighters." W. K. Moore, a Scottish lawyer practicing in Paso del Norte,
Mexico, hired the matadors and became their manager and press agent.

A cowboy had once bragged, "By nature, a Texas bull is all the time as
mean as he can get." That spurred the next mission. D. W. "Doc" Barton,
who had driven one of the first herds into Dodge, volunteered to procure the
meanest Texas Longhorns he could find and have them back in time for the
celebration.

The *Ford County Globe* printed the names and pedigrees of the twelve
Texas bulls. "Number one on the list was 'Ringtailed Snorter,' the oldest
and most noted of the twelve. He has been in twenty-seven different fights,
and always came off victor. Pedigree: Calved February 29, 1883; sire, Long

Cowtown officials spared no expense to provide entertainment for the trail-driving cowboys.
Dodge City Democrat, June 21, 1884

Mexican bullfighters traveled to Dodge City, Kansas, for the July 4th celebration of 1884.
Kansas State Historical Society

Horns; dam, All Fire, first of Great Fire, who won big money in a freeze-out at Supply in 1882." Ringtailed was joined by Iron Gall, Sheriff, Rustler, Loco Jim, and Eat-Em-Up Richard, among others. Betting began almost immediately.

Publicity and concerns for the upcoming event went wide and deep, so much so that it resulted in a letter to Dodge City's mayor from the US attorney. The missive advised that bullfighting was against the laws of the nation. The wire in reply read, "Hell, Dodge City ain't in the United States."

Numerous other events were planned for the celebration, including horse races, baseball games, shooting competition, and a traditional Texas roping event, which involved two riders on horseback with two ropes. The first to lasso, throw, and bind the cow in the shortest time wins. The *Kansas Cowboy* reported, "Play runs high and heavy bets are being made. It is indeed a gala season here, and a gala season at Dodge is unlikely to be witnessed elsewhere in the world."

The opening ceremony included a parade in which the guest matadors walked down Front Street to the newly constructed amphitheater. Local citizens and visitors, along with cowboys and their horses, lined both sides of the street to see the Mexican bullfighters. The five men wore red jackets, blue tunics, and white stockings. "They all seemed the perfection of litheness and quickness and were heartily applauded as their dark handsome faces looked on the crowd gathered along the streets," reports Mr. Taylor, special correspondent with the *St. Louis Globe-Democrat*.

The chief matador, Captain Gregorio Gallardo, carried two swords, one purported to be more than 150 years old and passed down from his grandfather, also a professional matador. The other toreros were picador Evaristo A. Rivas from Chihuahua and his son, Rodrigo Rivas. Professional musicians Marco Moya from Huejuequillo and Juan Herrerra from Aldama completed the cuadrilla.

Although newspaper articles of the day disparaged the wisdom of hosting such a spectacle, the event was considered a huge success and remains the only traditional Spanish bullfight ever held in the United States.

Glorified Beef Stew

The recipe collection of Wes Medley claims that Glorified Beef Stew was the dish served at A. B. Webster's saloon, in which the losing bulls gave their all after the fight. Advertised as the best stew served in the West, it does contain a unique combination of ingredients. I do not recommend bull meat, as it has a strong flavor and is tough. Any fine cut of beef will work.

Yield: 6–8 servings

Ingredients:

1 tablespoon lard

2 tablespoons olive oil

½ cup fat bacon, cooked and diced

2 onions, diced

A few carrots, sliced

2–3 tomatoes, sliced

2 pounds beef (stew, round, or sirloin), cut into cubes

Calf's foot, split in half

1 pint red wine

1 pint consommé or soup stock

A few sprigs of parsley

Some minced herbs

1 bay leaf

A few cloves

Salt

Pepper

Directions:

Put oil and lard in a large saucepan with the diced bacon, the sliced vegetables, the calf's foot, and the beef. When meat and vegetables begin to brown, add the wine, soup stock, herbs, and seasonings; bring to a boil. Cover saucepan and simmer very slowly for about 5 hours. May be eaten hot or cold, but must be served with the strained liquid over it. *Note:* If served cold, it should be placed in a mold, as the liquid will set into a jelly when cool.

Baked Bunkhouse Stew

An easy and flavorful baked stew from the QT Ranch in Butte, Montana, dated 1910. Leftovers heat up rich and tomatoey for a quick lunch, paired perfectly with a grilled cheese sandwich.

Yield: 6–8 servings

Ingredients:

2 pounds round steak (or pork)

4 tablespoons flour

2 teaspoons salt

¼ teaspoon pepper

2 tablespoons vegetable oil

1 cup sliced carrots

3 potatoes, peeled and quartered

1 cup chopped celery

2 cups tomato sauce

1 small can mushrooms, drained

1 cup water

6 small onions, quartered

Directions:

Cut steak into 1-inch cubes. In a mixing bowl, toss meat cubes with flour, salt, and pepper. Stir in oil, and mix until all pieces are moistened. Pour into a large casserole dish and add remaining ingredients. Cover dish with lid or foil and bake in oven at 350°F for about 2 hours.

"We had 4,500 head and we reached Dodge
City, Kansas, in fifty-five days."

A. E. SCHESKY, TRAIL DRIVER

Cow Camp Stew

As the herd moved slowly up the trail, the enterprising chuck wagon cook, with the trail boss's approval, would offer a trade with a local rancher's wife. In exchange for leaving behind a crippled steer, Cookie returned with garden-fresh vegetables such as potatoes, carrots, garlic, and onions, along with a few fresh eggs. The eggs rode safe under the wagon seat, nestled in the mule team's oats. Whatever the barter, this authentic recipe is proof that Cookie skillfully used what was on hand to create delicious fare from his rolling kitchen. For example, the ingredients in this stew may seem basic, but the flavor is bold, with subtle hints of coffee and molasses.

Yield: 4–6 servings

Ingredients:

1½ pounds lean beef for stewing, cut into 1½-inch cubes

2 tablespoons flour

½ teaspoon salt

2 tablespoons lard or shortening, melted

1½ cups strong coffee

2 tablespoons molasses

1 teaspoon Worcestershire sauce

1 clove garlic, crushed

½ teaspoon dried oregano

½ teaspoon salt

¼ teaspoon crushed red pepper

2 cups hot water

3 medium potatoes, diced

4 medium carrots, cut into ½-inch pieces

4 small onions, quartered

3 tablespoons flour

¼ cup cold water

Directions:

Combine first 2 tablespoons flour and ½ teaspoon salt; dredge beef in flour mixture, and brown in hot shortening in a Dutch oven. Stir in the next 7 ingredients and bring to a boil. Cover, reduce heat, and simmer 1½ hours, or until meat is tender. Add the 2 cups hot water and the vegetables. Cover and simmer 25 minutes, or until vegetables are tender. Combine the 3 table-spoons flour and ¼ cup water in a small bowl; stir until smooth. Gently stir flour mixture into stew; cover and simmer for 5 minutes.

Recipe for Chili—Family of Ten

A Valley Falls, Kansas, newspaper from 1907 reported: "There is a great craze for chili all over the country. In Kansas City a company has started a wholesale house and sells nothing but chili supplies. The restaurant people say that chili is a 'brain food.'" The recipe that follows was contributed to the January 1920 edition of the *Farmers Star and Livestock Inspector* magazine. The ingredients list is interestingly typical for chili that is served one hundred years later, and I love the wording in these instructions.

Yield: 10 servings

Directions:

I take 20 cents worth of chili meat chipped not too fine, take a nickel's worth of suet and fry out, discard the cracklins, then into this grease chop one large onion fine and one button of garlic and fry brown, but do not scorch; take the chopped meat and put into this, and mix all together and stir until all the meat turns white; then turn into a pot with three pound can of tomatoes; salt to taste and season with Gebhardt's chili powder. Have beans in another kettle boiled in water until soft. About one hour before serving and before seasoning add the beans, mash some of the beans to make body and use plenty of the powder. I have used this recipe for years and think it fine.

German born William Gebhardt introduced his bottled chili powder to the public in 1896 and was the first to market his product on a large scale, as evidenced by the recipe above from a Kansas newspaper. Importing fresh ancho peppers by the wagonload from San Potosi, Mexico, he discovered he could preserve the flavor for months by grinding dried chilies. He opened a factory in San Antonio and later published the first cookbook that focused on Mexican-American cooking in 1908.

Genuine Mexican Chili

Listed in a Kansas newspaper dated more than one hundred years ago, this recipe guarantees a "genuine Mexican chili recipe." The following is fine.

Yield: 4–6 servings

Directions:

Carefully wash and remove the stems from 12 large chili peppers. Pour over them a cup of boiling water, which will loosen the skins so they can be removed. Chop 1 small onion fine and put into a saucepan with 1 pound of nice, tender beef chopped fine while raw. Add 1 teaspoon lard and the same amount of suet. Let this mixture fry until well done. Then add a little salt, stir in the peppers chopped fine, add 1 quart of boiling water and cook 1 hour, stirring occasionally. Beans may be added if desired.

"Money is plentiful here, and consequently everyone is extravagant. One pays fifteen cents for a glass of lager beer and for other things in like proportion. The cowboy spends his money recklessly. He is a jovial careless fellow bent on having a big time regardless of expense. He will make way with the wages of a half year in a few weeks, and then go back to his herds for another six months."

KANSAS COWBOY NEWSPAPER, 1884

Cowtown Chili

Beans or no beans? The ongoing debate between chili lovers. This one adds the unique twist of refried beans, and I think you'll like it.

Yield: 6 servings

Ingredients:

1 pound ground beef
½ cup chopped onion
1 (16-ounce) can red beans
1 (16-ounce) can refried beans
1 (8-ounce) can tomato sauce
1 cup water
1 teaspoon chopped hot peppers
½ teaspoon salt
½ teaspoon garlic salt
⅛ teaspoon pepper
⅛ teaspoon cayenne
3 tablespoons chili powder
1 tablespoon molasses

Directions:

Brown beef with onions in a Dutch oven; drain fat. Add remaining ingredients; cover and simmer 1 hour, stirring occasionally.

"My first trip up the trail was in 1878 with Bob Martin from Refugio County with 1,100 two-year-olds and upwards. Our chuck wagon was drawn by two yoke of steers, and Adam Johnson, a negro, was our cook."

W. M. SHANNON, TRAIL DRIVER

Pickled Eggs and Red Beets

Popularized in the taverns and pubs of Europe, Western saloons also offered pickled eggs for patrons as a snack with their beer or whiskey. This recipe is from the Freidlein collection, credited to the Saddle Horn Saloon in Arizona.

Yield: 6 eggs

Ingredients:
2 cups (about 1 pound) young beets
¼ cup brown sugar
½ cup vinegar
½ cup cold water
½ teaspoon salt
Small piece of stick cinnamon
3–4 whole cloves
6 hard-cooked eggs

Directions:

Wash beets; cut off leaves and stems, leaving about 1 inch of the root end. Cook until tender. Drain and skin. Boil all remaining ingredients except the eggs together for 10 minutes. Let beets stand in this liquid for several days. Add whole, shelled, hard-cooked eggs to the liquid. Refrigerate for 2 or more days.

"I buried my spurs in 'em; that's about the last I remember."

TANK GIBSON, COWBOY

Sweet Beans

Tavia Vinson created this easy and flavorful side that we serve every year during branding week on the Sanford Ranch. It goes with just about everything and has become a favorite with our day-working crew.

Yield: 6–8 servings

Ingredients:
2 cans chili beans
1 medium onion, diced
1 jalapeño, diced
6 slices bacon, chopped
⅓ cup brown sugar
Dash of Worcestershire sauce

Directions:

Sauté onion, jalapeño, and bacon in a skillet until bacon is done. Combine this with the beans in a medium saucepan. Bring to a boil; reduce heat and simmer for 10 minutes. You can add more jalapeño for heat or more sugar for sweet, if desired.

Cowboys sort and load calves for shipping on the Sanford Ranch, Texas.
Natalie Bright

Potato Salad

Potato salad has been around for more than a century, as evidenced by this recipe dated 1882 from the *Dodge City Times*. Imagine eating this at a restaurant on North Front. Out the window you can watch the jostle of people, cowboys, horses, and every kind of wagon you could name pass by on the street. Never a dull moment in Cowtown.

Yield: 6–8 servings

Directions:
One quart of hot boiled potatoes cut into slices, a small onion, and an apple finely chopped, pepper and salt to taste, one tablespoonful of vinegar, three tablespoonfuls of olive oil; some chopped parsley. Mix these ingredients well together, and when perfectly cold serve upon a bed of fresh, crisp lettuce with a French Dressing. (See recipe for Cowtown French Dressing, page 92.)

"When it is remembered that this was accomplished in so short a time, notwithstanding the fact that every particle of material had to be brought from the East, and that, too, over a slow-moving railroad, it will be seen that energy and a determined will were at work."

JOSEPH MCCOY, CATTLE BARON

Ranch Potato Salad

A favorite with our cowboys at the Sanford Ranch, we serve it with barbecue brisket and pinto beans. It's even better the next day. Trust me.

Yield: 12 servings

Ingredients:
6 medium potatoes, scrubbed and washed
4 boiled eggs, diced
½ cup diced dill pickles
8 slices bacon, fried and crumbled
Salt, to taste
Pepper, to taste
1 cup real mayonnaise
1–2 tablespoons prepared mustard
1 medium onion, if desired
1–2 tablespoons pickle juice, as needed

Directions:

Wash and scrub potatoes really well; leave skin on. Place in a large saucepan, cover with water, and boil until tender, about 30 minutes. Boil eggs in another saucepan. Remove potatoes from heat; drain and cool. When cool, chunk into large mixing bowl. Add diced eggs and other ingredients. Add pickle juice to moisten if too dry. Refrigerate until ready to serve

Cook's note: Boil potatoes whole with the skin on; they do not absorb much water when cooking, whereas without the skin they tend to be more mushy and tasteless. You can also use baked potatoes. If you plan to have leftovers for the next day, do not use onion.

"The West was not slackish with its food. Line a person's ribs well and he will do his best for the cause."

RAMON ADAMS, COWBOY AND AUTHOR

Fresh Green Beans and New Potatoes

Garden-fresh, home-grown vegetables; there's nothing better—except for warm buttered corn bread to go with it. From the award winning C Bar C chuck wagon team, this is a popular side across several generations with many versions.

Yield: 6 servings

Ingredients:

6 new potatoes

2 pounds fresh green beans

5 slices bacon

2 tablespoons minced dried onions

1 teaspoon garlic powder

Salt and pepper, to taste

Directions:

Boil potatoes whole until done. Cool, then remove skins. Cut into chunks. Clean, string, and snap green beans; wash very well. Cover with water in a Dutch oven or large saucepan and bring to a boil. Let cook for about 30 minutes. Fry bacon; let cool and then break into pieces. When beans are almost done, add bacon, potatoes, dried onions, garlic, and salt and pepper to taste. Serve with corn bread.

Sweet Potato Casserole

This popular, traditional Southern dish has been altered to many different variations across so many kitchens. Why do we add sugar to sweet potatoes when they are already sweet, you ask? Ours is not to question why—ours is but to fill our plate.

Yield: 12 servings

Ingredients:

3 eggs, lightly beaten

3 cups mashed sweet potatoes

½ cup sugar

⅓ cup milk

1 tablespoon vanilla extract

½ cup melted margarine

For Topping:

1 cup brown sugar

⅔ cup flour

1 cup chopped pecans

½ cup butter or margarine

Directions:

Mix beaten eggs, sweet potatoes, sugar, milk, vanilla, and margarine together. Spoon into a buttered 13 x 9-inch casserole dish. For topping: Combine brown sugar, flour, pecans, and margarine by blending with a fork or your fingers. Sprinkle over the sweet potato mixture. Bake at 350°F for 30 minutes.

That hoss gave me a better merry-go-round ride
than yuh pay a nickel for at a carnival.

WHISKEY

Trail bosses wanted their cowboys to stay alert and ready for any kind of trouble, so drinking alcohol was usually prohibited during the drive. When they were off duty and hit Cowtown, that was another story.

Corn mash whiskey was distilled using grain, water, and yeast and then aged in barrels. The Cowtown version was probably not aged that long, however. It went by many names, depending on the proprietor: Red Eye, Coffin Varnish, Tarantula Juice, or Taos Lightnin'. Some saloons made their own house special, referred to as "overnight whiskey." Burnt sugar and tobacco juice were added to alcohol to create the desired amber color.

"Why, I kin get better likker by holdin' a bottle under a mare till she has to pee."

You could order a Cactus Wine, which was a head-spinning combination of peyote tea and Mexican tequila. Or try a Mule Skinner, an interesting mix of whiskey and blackberry liqueur. Whatever your poison, you could be guaranteed a good time in Cowtown.

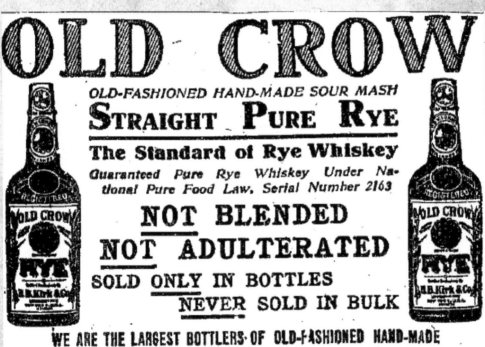

Advertisement for Old Crow in the December 31, 1909, edition of the *New York Times*
Wikimedia

Ol' Snakehead

I can imagine a group of Cowtown locals stirring up a batch of this in the alley behind the saloon. Drink it, if you dare.

Ingredients:

1 gallon alcohol

1 pound plug (black twist of tobacco)

1 pound molasses

1 handful Spanish peppers

5 gallons river water

2 rattlesnake heads per barrel for "spirit"

He was lappin' up likker like a fired cowhand.

Directions:

Mix in wooden barrels. Drop in a horseshoe. If the shoe sinks, the whiskey ain't ready; but when the shoe floats to the surface, the whiskey is ready to drink.

Whiskey Hot Toddy

There are numerous references to "toddy" in firsthand accounts about Cowtown, which I thought was interesting because my father made me a toddy when I had a sore throat. I can still remember that whiskey-fire burn all the way to my stomach. Plus the added lemon juice and honey sure stopped the coughing. A centuries-old classic that can be traced back to the Hindi word *taddy*, which means a beverage made of alcoholic liquor with hot water, sugar, and spices. If it ain't broke, don't fix it.

Yield: 1 serving

Ingredients:

Hot water

2 ounces whiskey

½ teaspoon sugar

Scrape of nutmeg

Directions:

Heat water to boiling in a saucepan or kettle. Measure whiskey into a tall mug. Fill mug to the top with hot water; spoon in sugar, stirring to blend. Grate nutmeg on top, if desired. Serve hot.

Spicy Hot Toddy

Yield: 1 serving

Ingredients:

Hot water
1 piece of sugar
1 piece of cinnamon
1 piece of lemon peel
4 cloves
1 jigger whiskey

He bowlegged it over to the bar to inoculate hisself agin' snake bites.

Directions:

Dissolve the sugar in a little hot water in a whiskey glass or tall mug. Add the other ingredients, and fill glass with hot water.

Whiskey barrels
Wikimedia

Traditional Whiskey Toddy

A Cowtown classic. Instead of white sugar, you can substitute brown sugar, honey, maple syrup, or agave nectar.

Yield: 1 serving

Ingredients:

½ teaspoon sugar
1 teaspoon water
1–2 ice cubes
6 ounces whiskey

Directions:

Place sugar in a whiskey glass; add water and stir. After the sugar is dissolved, add ice and then whiskey. Stir and enjoy.

> "I headed for a place across the street, where I could hear a fiddle. It was a saloon, gambling and dancing hall. Here I saw an old long-haired fellow dealing monte. I went to the bar and called for a toddy, and as I was drinking it a girl came up and put her little hand under my chin, and looked me square in the face and said, "Oh, you pretty Texas boy, give me a drink." I asked her what she wanted and she said anything I took, so I called for two toddies. My, I was getting rich fast—a pretty girl and plenty of whiskey."
>
> J. L. MCCALEB, TRAIL DRIVER

As more and more trade routes opened because of the increased reach by railroads to Kansas Cowtowns, patrons could enjoy more choices, including beer, brandy, a variety of wine, and even champagne. To increase inventory, the more expensive bourbon whiskey could be mixed with other ingredients.

Today there are two distinct spellings for this popular alcoholic beverage, depending on country of origin. Irish and American varieties are spelled "whiskey," with an "ey." Spelled with just a "y"—"whisky"—refers to products from Scotland, Canada, or Japan.

ABILENE, KANSAS: A WIDE-OPEN TOWN

The advertisement for the Bull's Head Saloon offended the most delicate citizenry of Abilene, no doubt about it. Historian J. Frank Dobie describes it as "a thoroughly masculine bull painted in red across the false front of his building." Abilene City Marshall Bill Hickok ordered tavern owners Phil Coe of Austin and Ben Thompson of Novia Scotia, England, to remove the offensive artwork. They refused.

Sharply dressed Thompson had a reputation as a gunman and professional gambler, and Hickok was one of his few friends. Coe was a known hothead and troublemaker, already at odds with the marshal because Hickok had accused him of cheating at cards.

Complaints from citizens and city councilmen mounted, and Marshal Hickok had no choice. Known to be tough but fair, Hickok exhibited a calm fearlessness that backed up his reputation. He hired painters to cover the offensive parts. Tensions between Coe and Hickok continued to build. Tensions between Abilene citizens and the drovers of those Texas longhorns had begun long before that.

A bronc buster from 1910
Wikimedia

"At Abilene, Kansas, we found a wide-open town. Ben Thompson and Hill Coe were running the noted Bull Head saloon, and Wild Bill Hickok was city marshal. There I met up with John Wesley Hardin, Buffalo Bill Thompson, Manny Clements and Gip Clements, and we went over to the gambling house. It did not take the gamblers there long to relieve me of all the money I possessed. Wild Bill Hickok told me that the best way to beat the game was to let it alone."

ALFRED IVERSON, TRAIL DRIVER

Beginning in 1867, when the Kansas Pacific Railroad arrived, and for the first three seasons as a Cowtown, Abilene had no organized police force. On the west bank of Mud Creek, the location began as a stop on the Butterfield Stage line. In his book *Historic Sketches of the Cattle Trade of the West and Southwest*, Joseph G. McCoy recalls, "Abilene in 1867 was a very small, dead place, consisting of about one dozen log huts, low, small, rude affairs, four-fifths of which were covered with dirt for roofing; indeed, but one shingle roof could be seen in the whole city." The well-watered river-bottom lands of the area were perfect for holding Texas longhorns and became an enticement for a year-round community of farming families as well. Conflicts between the two factions built as the population grew. "The Queen of Cowtowns" was also known as the "meanest hole in the state."

Clusters of agricultural communities strengthened in numbers—a group from Michigan, an Illinois colony, and the Buckeye township. Land agent, hustler, and Abilene mayor Theodore Henry envisioned "fenceless winter-wheat" fields. "When the time comes that these thousands and hundreds of thousands of cattle that are annually pouring in upon us," Henry declared, "retard the development of our county by deterring its settlement and cultivation—rather than contributing to its advancement, as perhaps they have done heretofore, then their presence should no longer be encouraged or tolerated here. Possibly I am mistaken, but my conviction is that that time is very near at hand."

The farmers pressured city electors for county herd laws to protect their property, while the cattlemen ignored them. Tensions mounted. Hickok's predecessor had been almost decapitated while serving a warrant. Interestingly, it was an ax-wielding Scottish homesteader instead of a Texas drover, but the year-round folks were growing more and more impatient.

Saloons and brothels were moved further away from the main townsite to an area called Fisher's addition, where fines and laws were loosely imposed. The fines collected from the saloons and good-time girls barely covered the cost of law enforcement.

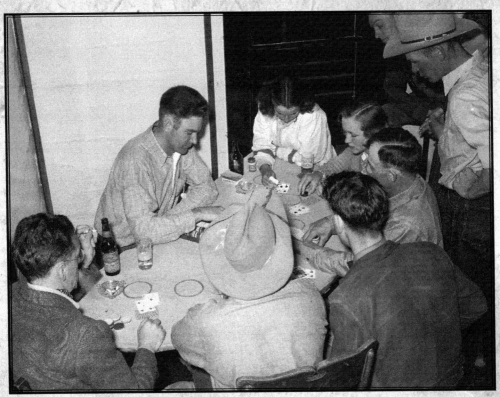

Cowboys and cowgirls play blackjack.
Library of Congress

February 1872. T. C. Henry issued a manifesto that was
circulated by the citizens of Abilene, Kansas, and mailed
to various Texas newspapers. It read as follows:

"We, the undersigned, members of the Farmer's Protective Association,
and officers and citizens of Dickinson county, Kansas, most respectfully
request all who have contemplated driving Texas cattle to Abilene
this coming Season to seek some other point for shipment, as the
inhabitants of Dickinson will no longer submit to the evils of the trade."

Rowdy Texas cowboys were to blame, because they also brought the gun-toters, gamblers, cutthroats, prostitutes, and other spreaders of sin seeking their share of the cash-flowing cattle business. Cowboys had even torn down their attempts to construct a city jail, which was finally completed under day-and-night guard.

In October 1871, Coe and Hickok's feud reached the boiling point. At the sound of gunshots, Marshal Hickok passed through the Alamo saloon into the street and asked who had fired the shot. Coe, who had been celebrating the end of the season with other Texas drovers since sundown, confessed that he had shot at a stray dog. Hickok drew his two ivory-handled revolvers, and the two men exchanged shots. When Deputy Williams approached in the shadows, Hickok spun and shot his friend twice. The deputy died almost instantly. Coe lingered for several days from his wounds before dying. Hickok was not injured. The season was over, and perhaps feelings died down a bit. However Marshal Hickok was fired, having served just one term as a Cowtown lawman.

The railroad had extended its reach to Newton, and that town willingly stepped in to welcome Texas drovers and their herds. That summer of 1871 had seen 50,000 Texas longhorns shipped by rail from the depot, and reportedly three times that number of head moved out on foot. It was the last cattle season for Abilene. The "courthouse ring" of land developers had gained victory in the election and were able to successfully spread their anti-cattle sentiment. The town suffered immediate decline, but Henry continued to realize much success, earning the title "the Wheat King of Kansas."

"The next town, Newton, Kansas, was a railroad camp as we went north and a big town when we came back through two months later, that being the terminus of the railroad at that time."

—GEORGE W. SAUNDERS, TRAIL DRIVER

WHERE THE WHEAT IS

DICKINSON WILL RAISE NEARLY 2,000,000 BUSHELS.

Farmers Say the Quality Will Be the Best in Many Years—Good Prices Assured.

Buffalo Bill Cody offered Hickok a place in his Wild West show after he lost his job as a lawman.
Library of Congress

The man with the initial vision, McCoy, observed that the cattle trade "was driven away by the schemes and concerted actions of a trio of office seekers." He moved to Wichita, Kansas.

Hickok left Cowtown country, gave up law enforcement, and never killed another man, perhaps because of a deep guilt after shooting his good friend. Other theories claim that he was losing his vision. He joined the traveling Wild West show with longtime friend Buffalo Bill Cody for a time but did not enjoy performing and was fired after only two months. While playing poker in Deadwood, South Dakota, he was shot in the back of the head and killed by a drunken gambler. Hickok was holding a black pair of aces and eights, now known as the Deadman's Hand.

Deadman's Hand
Natalie Bright

Roundup on the Sherman Ranch, Genesee, Kansas, ca. 1902.
Wikimedia

CHAPTER 5
GRAVIES AND SAUCES

"One hundred and fifty men for dinner at Bell's restaurant yesterday;
with six or eight other restaurants, and as many hotels and
boarding houses in the city, shows a pretty fair trade business."

FORD COUNTY GLOBE, APRIL 1885

Homemade Hot Sauce

Yield: About 4 (1-quart) jars

Ingredients:
3 quarts tomatoes, chopped
12 jalapeño peppers, chopped
4 large onions, chopped
Garlic, to taste
Salt, to taste
½ cup vinegar

Directions:

Mix all ingredients in a large saucepot and bring to a boil; simmer for about 1 hour, or until vegetables are done. Pour into hot jars and seal.

A modern-day Texas cowboy rides in flank position on a herd of bulls through mesquite trees, Sanford Ranch.
Natalie Bright

Basic White Sauce

A basic white sauce can be transformed into a variety of meals, such as a pasta sauce or combined with leftover meat and vegetables for an easy casserole. In ranch talk, it's simply cream gravy, and we use generous spoonfuls on everything from biscuits and eggs at breakfast to fried steak and mashed potatoes at dinner.

Yield: 1 cup sauce

Ingredients:
2 tablespoons butter or lard
2 tablespoons flour
1 cup milk

Directions:

Melt butter or lard. Add flour and stir quickly over low heat until smooth. Add milk and stir until thickened.

Easy Cheese Sauce

Yield: 6 cups

Ingredients:
¼ cup butter
¼ cup flour
5 cups milk
Salt, to taste
Pepper, to taste
¼ teaspoon nutmeg
¼ cup half-and-half
½ cup Parmesan cheese

Directions:

Melt butter in a large skillet. Add flour and allow it to bubble for 1–2 minutes, stirring with a whisk. Add milk and stir. Cook slowly at low heat for about 20–30 minutes. Add salt, pepper, and nutmeg to flavor. Stir in half-and-half and cheese. Serve over pasta. Add chunks of cooked vegetables, chicken, or shrimp if desired.

French Dressing

The term "French dressing" is referenced many times throughout recipes from the late 1800s. Many versions appeared in newspapers across the West. This one is the most popular and appears here as posted for subscribers.

Yield: 1 pint

Directions:

In a pint jar put one-fourth of a cup of vinegar and three-fourths of a cup of oil, a half teaspoon of salt, a little cayenne and a half teaspoon of pepper. Put on the rubber and the top of the jar and snap the wire fastening. Shake the jar rapidly up and down for a couple of minutes and a thick, perfectly blending French dressing is the result. Keep this in the jar in the ice box until needed, shaking it just before serving.

The term "ice box" literally means an ice box. It is a wooden, insulated piece of furniture with several doors; one cubby hole has a metal tray to hold a block of ice. Some communities harvested chunks of ice from the rivers when they froze over during the winter months. The block of ice was then stored in barns or underground bunkers and covered with hay or sawdust to slow the melting. Deliveries were made as needed to customers.

Chocolate Sauce

Yield: 2 cups

Ingredients:

1 cup chocolate chips
¾ cup water
¾ cup light corn syrup
½ cup sugar
¼ teaspoon salt
1 tablespoon butter
1 teaspoon vanilla

Directions:

In a 1-quart saucepan over low heat, melt chocolate in water, stirring until mixture is thick and smooth. Gradually stir in corn syrup, sugar, salt, and butter. Stirring constantly, bring to a boil. Off heat, stir in vanilla. Cool.

"We traveled due North for several days and saw many buffaloes. One day about noon they began going by and at six o'clock that evening they were still passing. Our horses stampeded at the sight of them and my brother had to follow them about eight miles before they could be overtaken and brought back."

A. F. CAMPBELL, TRAIL DRIVER

FRUIT PRESERVATION

Defined as pieces of fruit that are crushed or chopped, making jam out of fresh fruit and sugar or honey is an ancient method of preservation. Jelly is made from the strained juice of the fruit with the addition of pectin. The first recorded book of more than 500 recipes dates to fourth-century Rome.

Unique to the cattle driving ranges of the West are mesquite trees, which produce bean pods that were gathered by Native American tribes. The pods were ground into a flour using stone pestles or boiled whole for a beverage. The wood was used for tools, fencing, and corrals, and today you can find stunning pieces of furniture made from mesquite. More famous is mesquite-smoked beef barbecue in Texas, as well as several mesquite beverages such as vodka and coffee.

Mesquite Bean Jelly

The taste is sweet with a faint nuttiness; plus it's just fun making something that's been around for centuries. This recipe comes from one of our ranching neighbors, Chris Ingram. Next time you are traveling through the Midwest during June, you may notice these trees thick with beans. Watch out for the thorns!

Yield: 4–4½ pint jars

Ingredients:

2 gallons mesquite beans
2 lemons
4½ cups reserved juice
¼ cup lemon juice
1 box fruit pectin
7 cups sugar

Directions:

Pick mesquite beans when they turn red. (Long straight beans turn red; curly beans do not.) Clean and wash beans, removing stems and leaves. In a 20-quart stainless steel pot, place about 2 gallons of beans and the rinds of the 2 lemons. Cover with water by 2 inches. (It is advisable to cook outside, as the mixture has a very strong smell when cooking.) Bring to a boil and simmer with lid on for at least 1 hour. Drain off juice and reserve; discard beans. In a 10-quart pot add reserved juice from the beans, lemon juice, and pectin. Bring to rolling boil and cook for 1 minute. Add sugar and bring back to a rolling boil; cook for 5 minutes. Pour into jars and seal.

Bread Pudding Sauce

Yield: 1½ cups

Ingredients:
1 cup sugar
¼ cup flour
½ teaspoon salt
1 cup milk
1 egg, beaten
1½ tablespoons butter
1 teaspoon vanilla

Directions:

In a medium saucepan, combine sugar, flour, and salt. Gradually add milk, stirring constantly to keep it smooth. Heat over low heat until mixture begins to thicken. Add a small amount of sauce to beaten egg and stir well, then add egg to cooked mixture. Cook until desired thickness. Remove from heat; cool and stir in butter and vanilla. Pour over bread pudding.

Vanilla Sauce

A basic and simple flavor that pairs well with puddings, cakes, or fruit. Especially delicious on bread pudding.

Yield: 1¾ cups

Ingredients:
½ cup butter
1 cup sugar
½ cup heavy whipping cream
1½–2 teaspoons vanilla extract

Directions:

In small saucepan over medium-low heat, melt the butter. Add the sugar, whipping cream, and vanilla, stirring constantly until the sugar is dissolved and the mixture has a syrup consistency. Serve warm. Sauce will thicken as it cools.

Ace High Barbecue Sauce

Yield: 5 cups

Ingredients:
1 cup strong black coffee
1 cup Worcestershire sauce
1 cup catsup
½ cup cider vinegar
½ cup brown sugar
3 tablespoons chili powder
2 teaspoons salt
2 cups chopped onion
¼ cup minced hot chili peppers
6 cloves garlic, minced

Directions:

Combine all ingredients in a saucepan and simmer 25 minutes. Strain or puree in a blender or food processor. Store in the refrigerator.

We camped with our herd about six miles south of Dodge City, on Mulberry Creek. The first thing we did when we arrived there was to go to town, get a shave and haircut, and tighten our belts by a few good strong drinks.

GEORGE GERDES, TRAIL DRIVER

Barbecue Sauce

This long list of ingredients comes together perfectly, and it's good for basting or as a side for grilled meats.

Yield: 2 cups

Ingredients:

1 medium onion, chopped

2 tablespoons butter

2 tablespoons vinegar

2 tablespoons brown sugar

4 tablespoons lemon juice

1 cup catsup

½ cup water

½ tablespoon prepared mustard

3 tablespoons Worcestershire sauce

¼ teaspoon salt

¼ teaspoon cayenne pepper

¼ teaspoon crushed red pepper

Directions:

Brown onion in butter. Add remaining ingredients. Simmer 30 minutes, then pour over beef, pork ribs, or goat.

Leonard Restaurant—F. J. Leonard

Fred is a caterer of the highest order. His restaurant is finely furnished in table ware, cutlery, &c. He is an accommodating, sociable and affable gentleman and has a first-class patronage. His table is furnished with the finest the market affords, and the most fastidious palate or the epicure can satiate their appetites at his board.

Mr. Leonard furnishes fresh oysters in season, and he serves them up in every style.

Leonard's large dining hall is well furnished and attractive, and his accommodations being ample, he can serve parties on the shortest notice with a meal gotten up in the finest style of the culinary art.

The charges are reasonable and satisfaction given.

DODGE CITY TIMES, 22 DECEMBER 1877

Medley's Special Barbecue Sauce

This includes a long and varied list of ingredients, but it's worth the trouble.

Yield: 3 cups sauce

Ingredients:

1 cup butter
¼ cup vinegar
1 tablespoon sugar
2¼ teaspoons chili powder
1½ teaspoons Worcestershire sauce
¼ teaspoon pepper
1 tablespoon minced onion
2½ cups beef stock
1¼ teaspoons dry mustard
2 teaspoons salt
Dash cayenne pepper
½ teaspoon Tabasco
1 tablespoon paprika
1 garlic clove

Directions:

Combine all ingredients in a medium-sized saucepan. Boil for 20 minutes; remove garlic clove. Use to baste pork, beef, or chicken as it broils. To baste, tie a clean cloth on the end of a long stick; dip the cloth in the sauce and juices, and rub it on the meat. Do this constantly while cooking. Keep turning the meat so it broils evenly.

We crossed at Red River Station and arrived at Newton, Kansas, about the time the railroad reached there. Newton was one of the worst towns I ever saw, every element of meanness on earth seemed to be there.

L. B. ANDERSON, TRAIL DRIVER

Riding in the point man position, this cowboy determines the direction and speed of the drive. Sanford Ranch, Texas.

Natalie Bright

1855-Style Sauce

Sweet and savory. Perfect for baked chicken, ham, lamb, or pork roast.

Yield: 2½ cups sauce

Ingredients:
1 cup Southern Comfort (whiskey)
2 tablespoons grated orange rind
¼ cup honey
¼ cup soy sauce
1 cup orange juice
2 cloves garlic, crushed
1 tablespoon cornstarch

Directions:

Combine all ingredients. Pour into a saucepan and bring to a boil. Lower heat and simmer for 12 minutes, stirring constantly. Let cool. Freeze leftovers.

HOLE-IN-THE-WALL PASS

Rustlers presented a huge problem for trailing herds. Cattle that did not make it to the Cowtown railhead was money lost for all involved and no beef to fulfill the demand back East. In the North, livestock stolen from their new-pasture homes proved devastating for ranching families. About seven miles from Dodge City, Horse Thief Canyon was the preferred hideout. Livestock could be hidden there until rewards were announced; then the cattle would be "found" and the rustlers would collect.

A remote and popular place for cattle rustlers and outlaws, Hole-in-the-Wall hideout was located in the Big Horn Mountains of Johnson County, Wyoming. Approachable only through a narrow gorge, a pass led up the mountainside, where numerous log cabins, a livery stable, and a corral were built. Each gang provided their own supplies and carried out their own robberies. The pass was the perfect place for wintering and as a base of operations, and outlaw gangs frequented it from the 1860s to around 1910. Lawmen were never able to penetrate the hideout during its time of use.

"Fort Worth Five." Front row left to right: Harry A. Longabaugh, alias the Sundance Kid; Ben Kilpatrick, alias the Tall Texan; Robert Leroy Parker, alias Butch Cassidy. Standing: Will Carver and Harvey Logan, alias Kid Curry.
Wikimedia

According to legend, the outlaws never robbed the nearby ranchers, always paying for any supplies or livestock they needed.

One well-known gang operated out of Hole-in-the-Wall and committed frontier crimes across the four-state area. Their leader was the son of a devout Mormon farmer. Known by most as Butch Cassidy, he was described by some as being "cheery and affable" and only shot at the horses not the man, while others claimed he had an uncontrollable temper and killed for vengeance. Under his leadership the notorious Hole-in-the-Wall Gang grew to 500 marauders who spread devastation to the ranching families and frontier towns throughout Utah, Colorado, Idaho, and Wyoming. Rustled cattle were driven through Colorado and into Mexico. In addition, they robbed trains, banks, and company payrolls. It was the Pinkerton detectives and a group of gunfighters organized by the railroad that eventually encouraged Butch to relocate his operations to South America.

Included in the collection of cowboy cook Wes Medley are authentic recipes from the cooks at Wyoming's famed Hole-in-the-Wall hideout. Wes inherited the recipes from his great-uncle Freidlein, who once employed a ranch hand who claimed to have been a gang member that frequented the pass.

Hole-in-the-Wall Stew

Directions:

Kill off a young steer or sheep. Cut up the heart, sweetbread, kidneys, brains, and liver. Also cut off the marrow gut from either the calf or sheep. Cut into 1-inch pieces. Put into hot fat in a Dutch oven or kettle and cook until browned. Depending on how hot the stove is, it might take ½ to 1 hour. Then add the rest of the cut-up meat. Add salt, pepper and garlic to taste, or even a little hot chili powder. It takes about 3 hours to cook. About ½ hour to 45 minutes before the stew is done, you can also add potatoes, cooked beans, or rice.

Hole-in-the-Wall Fat Back or Salt Pork

Directions:

Slice pork rather thick, or thin, depending on the cook. Dampen the pork with water and roll in a mixture of flour and cornmeal. Put in a skillet with a little lard and fry until done. Good with pork gravy and fried cornmeal bread.

Hole-in-the-Wall Gravy

Directions:

Put ½ handful flour into hot pork grease left in skillet. Keep stirring until the flour gets real dark and smokes up the cabin. Gravy ain't good unless it's burned. Then stir like hell and add water until you get the right thickness. Add salt and pepper. Serve hot with corn cakes.

Hole-in-the-Wall Cornmeal Cakes

Ingredients:
4–6 good handfuls of cornmeal
2 large tablespoons lard
Couple pinches of salt and pepper
Cap lid full of vinegar
Couple pinches of brown sugar

Directions:

Mix all this together and pour enough boiling water over to make a thick batter. Fry in a skillet. Good with anything.

Hole-in-the-Wall Biscuits

Ingredients:
3 handfuls flour
8 pinches baking powder
1 pinch salt
1 pinch sugar
3 big spoonfuls lard
1 cup water

The man that always straddles the fence usually has a sore crotch.

Directions:

Mix together all dry ingredients. Mix in lard until flaky. You might need a little extra water to moisten. Put on a floured table; pat out to the desired thickness. Place in a greased Dutch oven that has been slightly heated. Place lid on oven and cook with hot coals. Let bake about 20 minutes until brown on both ends. Can also be used in a cook stove.

Day-working cowboys waiting for their turn to rope at spring branding. Sanford Ranch, Texas.
Natalie Bright

CHAPTER 6

SWEETS

"Their language may not always have been couched in terms accepted of
the church. Their prayers may not have always been as dignified, or their
hymns as pure in tone as they might have been, but within the breasts
of the men who braved the hardships of those early days beat hearts
as true as those which beat within the breasts of any God's Children."

CHAPLAIN J. STEWART PEARCE, FIRST INFANTRY, CAMP TRAVIS

Bread Puddings

A longtime staple for frugal housewives and restaurants for decades, bread pudding remains the tastiest use of stale leftovers. As one newspaperman observed in the *Chelsea Reporter* (1911): "Restaurant and hotel keepers who still serve bread pudding do so in a sneaking manner and give it an assumed name such as, 'cabinet pudding, succulent sauce,' 'Coburg pudding,' 'favorite food,' and so on and serve it in thick cups as they do whiskey up in Maine." He was right in his assumption. This classic dessert appears on many Cowtown menus. Here are a few versions from Nellie Maxwell as shared in the *Leavenworth Post* (1911), printed here as it appeared in her article more than a century ago.

"Bread pudding is not one to be despised, for it is both wholesome and appetizing when well made, and one always feels so virtuous when something good is made out of material that many throw away." The following are a few of the many good ones to try.

Bread Crumb Pudding

Directions:

Soak half a pint of breadcrumbs in one pint of sweet milk; add the yolks of two eggs, half a cup of sugar, a tablespoon of butter and any flavoring desired. Mix well and add a few raisins and bake one hour. Cover with a meringue, using the whites of the eggs and sugar. Bake a light brown.

Chocolate Bread Pudding

Directions:

Scald two cups of milk and pour over two cups of bread crumbs; melt one square of chocolate over hot water. Dip out a little of the milk, add to the chocolate with a third of a cup of sugar. Add an egg, beaten; add the crumbs and flavoring desired and bake in a moderate oven thirty minutes. Serve warm with a sauce made by creaming a half cup of butter and adding a cup of sugar and flavoring to taste.

Queen of Puddings

Directions:

Mix together a pint of milk and a pint of bread crumbs and a cup of sugar, the yolks of two eggs, a tablespoonful of melted butter and the rind of a lemon. Bake slowly a half hour, then remove and spread with jam, jelly or preserves, and cover with meringue made of the whites of the eggs, a half cup of sugar and the juice of the lemon. Cover the pudding and brown. Serve with or without cream.

A Delicious Bread Pudding

Directions:

Butter several slices of bread and lay in the bottom of a baking dish; pour any stewed sauce, like prunes, peaches or canned fruit, then another layer of bread and bake with or without a meringue. This may be eaten with cream and sugar for a sauce or, if the fruit is juicy, it will need none.

Cowgirl, Newton, Kansas
Bain News Service, Library of Congress

C-Bar-C Bread Pudding

From the award-winning C-Bar-C chuck wagon cooking team of Sue Cunningham and Jean Cates, here is another bread pudding recipe.

Yield: 12–20 servings, depending on serving size

Ingredients:

4 eggs

1½ cups sugar

1 teaspoon vanilla

½ teaspoon cinnamon

6 large biscuits or rolls (6 slices bread)

1 (12-ounce) can evaporated milk

½ can water (6 ounces)

¾ cup raisins (optional)

½ teaspoon nutmeg

2–3 tablespoons butter

Directions:

Mix eggs, sugar, vanilla, and cinnamon; beat well. Tear bread into small pieces; add to egg mixture. Add evaporated milk and water to egg mixture and beat well. Add raisins if desired. Let set 5–10 minutes to allow bread to soften. (If it seems too dry, add more water.) Pour into a greased 9 x 13 or 10 x 10 x 2-inch pan. Sprinkle nutmeg over top, if desired. Dot with butter. Bake at 350°F for 30–45 minutes. Will be jiggly in the center. Do not overcook.

"The dough wrangler would make up a mess of them apple dumplings after dinner. The only thing wrong with 'em was that we didn't get 'em often enough."

MARION HILGER, TRAIL DRIVER

Whiskey Sauce for Bread Pudding

Yield: 1 cup sauce

Ingredients:

½ cup butter

1½ cups powdered sugar

1 egg yolk

½ cup Bourbon whiskey

Directions:

Heat butter and sugar over medium heat until all butter is absorbed. Remove from heat and blend in egg yolk. Pour bourbon in gradually, stirring constantly. The sauce will thicken as it cools.

Drover's Hotel opposite the stockyards, Kansas City, Kansas
Library of Congress

COWBOY GEAR

The trailing drover had a unique dress all his own. While the chuck wagon served as his address where he ate and slept, everything else he needed for the job was carried with him on his horse. The horse was just as completely outfitted as the rider.

A cowboy's most prized possession is his saddle. The original design originated from the Mexican vaquero, with changes through the years to the riggin', horn style, and placement of the cinch. Navajo blankets were the favored padding under the saddle to protect the horse's back. The colors and designs were eye-catching, and the tightly-woven wool absorbed sweat. The headstall, bridle, bit, and reins outfitted the rest of a cowboy's mobile workstation.

The most important tool in a wrangler's gear was a "ketch rope," its primary purpose being to catch and hold horses or cows. Early materials used included fibers of the century plant, and cowboys called the rope a "McGay." The "manila" is a woven three-strand manila fiber. A "grass rope" could be waterproofed by mixing beef tallow with melted paraffin. Twisted linen and cotton were apt to stretch and fray. Rawhide ropes could be made from buffalo or cattle hide, called "skin strings." Hair from the horse's mane and tail were braided into ropes but often too light to throw. Horsehair made good lead or tie ropes.

Humans dress up but the cowboy dresses down.

Branding with a hot iron continues to be the best way to identify livestock ownership.
Natalie Bright

Every piece of a trailing cowboy's clothing served a purpose from the hat on his head, the bandana around his neck, to the special boots he wore. Handmade and made to order, the boot's toe had to be pointed for slipping into the stirrup easily—and for slipping out if he was thrown. The tops were at around seventeen inches high to protect his shins from scratchy mesquite brush thorns and stirrup leathers, as well as rocks and dirt thrown up by the horse's hooves. The soles were slick, durable leather, and the heels were high, narrow, and undersloped to catch the stirrup firmly. He rode with his weight on the arch. "Mule ears" were leather pulls that provided ease for the wearer to shove his foot into his boots quickly. Loyalty to the bootmaker was everything as long as they fit tight and right. They were not the best footwear for walking or dancing.

Detail of a man's blue jeans, boots, and spurs.
Pie Town, New Mexico
Library of Congress

In Abilene, Kansas, Tom C. McInerney set up his boot shop, employing as many as twenty men during the summer. He offered a unique design with red tops and tooled Lone Stars and crescent moons.

John C. Mueller moved from Ellsworth, where he was already successful as a boot maker, to partner with Walter Straeter in Dodge City. Their shop on Front Street carried the largest stock of shop-made boots. Their success propelled them into opening the large and impressive Old House saloon.

The actual design for the cowboy boot is credited to shoemaker Charles H. Hyer, who worked as the foreman of the shoe shop at the State Institution for the Deaf in Olathe, Kansas. In 1881 he and his brother opened a little shop where one day a cowboy rode up to inquire if they could make a pair of boots. After discarding the first two attempts, Hyer is credited with the design and style of the first boots for the trail-riding cowboy. That little shop grew to be the largest manufacturer of handmade cowboy boots in America.

A cowboy's gear remains much the same as in the old days. It may be made with completely different material, but the uses of the gear and purpose of the work have remained the same for more than a century.

"In those days I received $30 a month, furnished three horses and had money at the end of the trip. Our way back home was paid by those who employed us. We came back as immigrants, all dressed up in new suit, boots and hat, the rig out costing about $30, and when we reached home we were "somebody come" sure enough, as we were usually absent about four months."

R. J. JENNINGS, TRAIL DRIVER

Spotted Pup

A tasty twist on a chuck wagon staple. Cookie did not have eggs or milk on the chuck wagon, so I was pleasantly surprised to discover a town version of this cowboy favorite. It's just as tasty as the authentic dish that was served fireside in cow camp.

Yield: 4 servings

Ingredients:
2 cups milk
3 eggs
1 cup sugar
1 teaspoon vanilla
1 teaspoon cinnamon
1 teaspoon nutmeg
1 cup raisins
2 cups leftover cooked rice

Directions:

Heat milk to boiling in a large saucepan; reduce heat. Slightly beat together eggs, sugar, and vanilla. Stir mixture into milk until smooth. Add remaining ingredients. Pour into Dutch oven or casserole dish. Bake at 375°F for 25 minutes, until knife inserted in center comes out clean.

A cowboy without a horse is just a man in a hat.
Library of Congress

Shoo-Fly Pie

With origins traced back to the Pennsylvania Dutch, the name comes from the smooth and sweet filling that probably attracted those pesky insects.

Yield: 1 pie

Ingredients:

1 unbaked pastry shell
½ cup dark molasses
½ cup boiling water
½ teaspoon baking soda
1 large egg

For crumb mixture:

¼ cup shortening
2 cups flour
½ cup brown sugar
Dash of salt
¼ teaspoon cinnamon

Directions:

Prepare 1 unbaked pastry shell. Mix together molasses, boiling water, baking soda, and egg. Pour into pie shell. Top with Crumb Mixture, made by cutting shortening into the dry ingredients listed above. Bake 1–1¼ hours at 350°F.

"From 1875 to 1882 I suppose I had more experience, good and bad, than any one man on the trail with Indians, buffalo, horse rustlers, and cutthroats, and during that time I worked eighteen hours out of every twenty-four. Wound up in 1882 without a dollar in hand, but in possession of several thousand dollars' worth of fun."

GUS BLACK, TRAIL DRIVER

Pecan Cream Pie

A traditional pecan pie with milk in the filling and a meringue topping—delicious and unexpected. The instructions for a baked beaten egg white and sugar confection first appeared in a manuscript book by Lady Elinor Fettiplace dated 1604.

Yield: 1 pie

Ingredients:

1 cup sugar

3 heaping tablespoons flour

¼ teaspoon salt

1½ cups milk

1 tablespoon butter

3 egg yolks, beaten

½ cup chopped pecans

1 teaspoon vanilla

1 baked pie shell

For meringue topping:

3 egg whites

¼ teaspoon baking powder

6 tablespoons sugar

Directions:

For pie filling: Combine all ingredients except pie shell together in a medium saucepan and cook until thick, stirring constantly. Add vanilla and pour into baked pie shell.

For meringue topping: Beat egg whites. Add baking powder and sugar, 1 tablespoon at a time, after the egg whites start looking foamy. Beat until stiff peaks form. Spread meringue on pie filling. Seal meringue to crust and bake at 350°F for 12–15 minutes, or until golden brown.

Old-Fashioned Tea Cakes

Yield: 3 dozen

Ingredients:

1 cup sugar

½ cup lard (or shortening)

1 egg

1 teaspoon vanilla

1 teaspoon nutmeg

1 teaspoon baking powder

½ teaspoon baking soda

½ teaspoon salt

3 cups flour

½ cup buttermilk

Directions:

Mix sugar, lard, eggs, and vanilla together. Sift flour, baking powder, soda, and salt together; add alternately with buttermilk. Roll out on floured board and cut with a biscuit cutter. Bake on a greased cookie sheet at about 315°F for 10–12 minutes.

"Put a cowman a foot and he don't know a thing."

RAMON ADAMS

Carrot Cake

With a garden full of fresh vegetables, why not figure every way possible to use them?

Yield: 1 tube pan or 2 loaf pans

Ingredients:

2 cups sugar

4 eggs

1½ cups oil

3 cups flour

2 teaspoon baking soda

½ cup buttermilk

2 teaspoons cinnamon

1 cup chopped pecans

3 cups grated carrots

1 cup powdered sugar

1 teaspoon lemon extract

3 tablespoons orange juice

Directions:

Cream sugar, eggs, and oil. Into mixture, blend flour, baking soda, and buttermilk; add cinnamon. Stir in pecans, carrots, and lemon extract, mixing well. Bake in a tube pan at 300°F for 1½ hours, or bake in two loaf pans for 35–45 minutes. Cool. Cover with glaze of powdered sugar and orange juice to spread.

A good cowboy can stay awake all summer and
catch up on his sleep in the winter.

Chocolate Pound Cake

Dating back to the 1700s, pound cake is thought to have originated as so named because of the easy-to-remember ingredients—1 pound each of flour, butter, eggs, and sugar—and it feeds a lot of people. Today's versions may be smaller and lighter, but the name still stands.

Yield: 1 tube pan or 2 loaf pans

Ingredients:

1 cup butter

½ cup shortening

3 cups sugar

5 eggs

1 teaspoon vanilla extract

3 cups flour

½ teaspoon baking powder

½ teaspoon salt

4 tablespoons cocoa

1 cup milk

Directions:

Cream together butter and shortening. Add sugar and mix well. Add eggs, one at a time, beating after each. Add vanilla. Combine dry ingredients and add alternately with milk to creamed mixture. Bake in a greased 10-inch tube pan at 325°F for 80 minutes or two loaf pans at the same temperature for 35–45 minutes.

"Most of his meals tasted like they were boiled from hoof-trimmin's, but he could sure bake them after-meal sweets!"

JOHN HUNTER, TRAIL DRIVER

Hard Candy

A sweet treat that can be carried in a cowboy's saddlebags or pocket.

Yield: 10 dozen

Ingredients:
2 cups molasses
2 cups brown sugar
½ teaspoon vinegar

Directions:

Place ingredients in a pan over medium heat. Just as the mixture begins to boil, strain well. Return to heat and boil until a bit of the mixture becomes brittle when dropped in cold water. Immediately pour onto a greased baking sheet. Grease or flour your hands so you can handle the candy. Pull it up from the sheet and then pull into a long stick shape. Score with a greased knife every 1 inch or so. When cool, the candy will break at those scored lines.

Sugar Candy

Dated 1919 from the plains of North Dakota, candy "strings" when the syrup drips from a spoon and forms thin threads in cold water.

Yield: 2 dozen

Ingredients:
2 cupfuls of maple sugar
1 to 2 pints of cream
1 cupful of nuts

Directions:

Boil the sugar and cream together until it strings. Then beat thoroughly and add the nuts. Lay on a buttered pan, and cut in blocks. ***Note:*** Maple sugar was prepared from the sap of a maple tree and popular throughout Canada and the Northeast.

"We found the best use for his candy was for lure'n yer horse first thing in the morning."

BILL CRAIG, TRAIL DRIVER

Crazy Cake

Using basic ingredients you have on hand, this is a simple cake loaded with flavor. Note the interesting method used to mix the cake in the same pan used for baking.

Yield: 1 cake

Ingredients:

1½ cups flour

1½ cups sugar

½ cup cocoa

2 teaspoons baking soda

½ teaspoon salt

⅔ cup cooking oil

1 teaspoon vanilla

2 teaspoons vinegar

2 cups cold, strong coffee or cold water

For topping:

½ cup sugar

½ teaspoon cinnamon

Directions:

Sift all dry ingredients together into an ungreased 13 x 9 x 2-inch metal baking pan. Stir together well with a fork. Make three wells in the flour mixture; pour oil into one, vinegar in one, and vanilla in the other. Pour cold coffee over all ingredients. Stir with a fork until well blended. Do not overbeat. For the topping, combine sugar and cinnamon; sprinkle over the batter. Bake in 350°F oven for 35-40 minutes.

"In June 1869 my father trailed a herd of twenty-five hundred cattle to Los Angeles, California, being on the trail about eight months."

MARY TANKERSLEY LEWIS, DAUGHTER OF A TRAIL DRIVER

Custard Pie

This familiar, old-fashioned pie comes from the Wild Cow Chuck Wagon Cooking Team. It's been a favorite for several generations, and I love the note about scalding milk. Not everyone is lucky enough to have a milk cow.

Yield: 1 pie, 6–8 servings

Ingredients:
3 eggs
1 cup sugar
2 tablespoons flour
1 cup milk
1 teaspoon vanilla
½ teaspoon nutmeg
9-inch pie shell

Directions:

Brush empty pie shell with egg whites before filling. No need to scald milk that is pasteurized. Combine all ingredients and blend until smooth. Pour into unbaked pie shell and bake at 400°F for 35–40 minutes.

"We spent three months on the road to hell at twenty dollars a month only to spend it in less than a week on whiskey and women."

JIM LARDER, TRAIL DRIVER

UNION PACIFIC HOTEL, ABILENE, KANSAS

UNION PACIFIC MENU.

Following is the Bill of Fare for the Union Pacific Hotel
Dinner, tomorrow, April 11, '97

Pot au Feu

~

Baked Catfish, au court bouillon
A la Duchess Potatoes

~

Boiled Sugar Cured Ham and Cabbage

~

Roasted Turkey, English dressing, cranberry sauce
Roast Sirloin of Beef, pan gravy
Roast Spring Lamb, caper sauce

~

Baked Chicken Pie, southern style
Pork Spare Ribs, with sauer kraut
Calf Brain Patties, cream sauce
Baked Spaghetti and Cheese
Banana Fritters, strawberry sauce

~

French Slaw. Salmon Salad.

~

Mashed Potatoes
Sweet Corn. French Peas. New Beans.

~

Graham Bread. White Bread.

~

Chocolate Ice Cream
Cherry Pie. Apple Meringue Pie.
Nesserole Pudding, brandy sauce.

~

Assorted Cake. Layer Raisins.
Edam Cheese. Sweet Clover Brick Cheese.
Java Coffee. Tea. Iced Tea. Sweet Milk. Buttermilk.
Sand Springs Water

The Celebrated Belle Springs Creamery Butter Served at all Meals.

Apple Meringue Pie

A nice variation for traditional apple pie.

Yield: 1 (9-inch) pie

Ingredients:

7 cups peeled, thinly sliced tart apples

2 tablespoons lemon juice

⅔ cup sugar

2 tablespoons flour

⅓ cup whole milk

2 large egg yolks, beaten

1 teaspoon grated lemon zest

Pastry for single-crust pie (9 inches)

1 tablespoon butter

For meringue:

3 large egg whites

¼ teaspoon cream of tartar

6 tablespoons sugar

Directions:

In a large bowl, toss apples with lemon juice. In a small bowl, whisk sugar, flour, milk, egg yolks, and lemon zest until smooth. Pour over apples and toss to mix. Line a 9-inch pie plate with pastry; trim to ½ inch beyond edge of pie plate and flute edges. Pour filling into crust; dot with butter. Cover edges loosely with foil. Bake at 400°F for 20 minutes. Remove foil; bake 25–30 minutes longer, or until apples are tender. Reduce heat to 350°F. In a bowl, beat the egg whites and cream of tartar on medium speed until foamy. Gradually beat in sugar, 1 tablespoon at a time, on high just until stiff peaks form and sugar is dissolved. Spread evenly over hot filling, sealing edges to crust. Bake for 15 minutes, or until meringue is golden brown. Cool on a wire rack. Store in the refrigerator.

GAMBLERS AND GOOD-TIME GIRLS

Chisholm Trail

You strap on your chaps, your spurs, and your gun—
You're goin' into town to have a little fun.
You play with a gambler who's got a marked pack;
You walk back to camp with your saddle on your back.

The economic stability of Cowtowns relied on another important group of transients other than the trail driving cowboys. Gamblers and prostitutes beat a path westward that led to the sleepy little settlements bursting with Texas longhorns. No doubt this group possessed skills that provided much-needed entertainment and diversion to entice the cattle barons and drovers away from their cash.

What began in tents or shacks with crude bars made from a plank laid across two barrels soon led to chic interiors of polished brass and rows of gambling tables. Nude paintings of buxom beauties with coy smiles hung behind intricately carved bars. Advertising only the best in fine dining and accommodations, a multitude of establishments such as dance halls, saloons, and hotels lined the dusty streets. The signs of a more prosperous community could not be denied by the locals.

A giant wheel of fortune or card games such as poker, monte, and faro could be found in most every establishment. Fast-action games of chance such as keno, craps, and roulette were exciting enough to match the live-or-die experiences of the trail-weary cowboys. In short, wagering was a popular past time in the Old West, and almost everybody gambled.

Dressed in style with jovial personalities, professional gamblers became respected citizens and often returned every season in early spring with the arrival of the first herds. Saloon owners allowed the high rollers to set up independent businesses or put them on the payroll to run the gaming tables. Some gamblers put down roots and opened their own establishments. These sharply dressed gamers made the most of their money in volume, running multiple games with various players throughout the night rather than playing for huge stakes. There were limits on bets. Poker had a $1 to $2 limit, and faro cost 25 cents to $1 to gain a seat at the table.

Close on the heels of the transient gamblers, the good-time girls arrived in droves. Their stories and reasons were varied. Some, having been abandoned by husbands, wanted a fresh start; others were escaping abusive situations, and their only option for survival was turning to the quickest means necessary. The story is told that two well-known schoolteachers realized the local "soiled doves" made more in a week in Cowtown than they did all year teaching, so they took up part-time work during the summers.

There were many hands in the till at the expense of the frail sisters, along with a recognizable caste system. Like the professional gamblers, they arrived in spring and left in early fall, following the last trainload of long-horns to spend winters back East. Some went the opposite direction though, traveling further west to find new opportunities in burgeoning cities in the Rocky Mountains or Sacramento Valley.

Trail driver E. C. Abbott, "Teddy Blue," recalls: "There are girls there that I had seen at a lot of different places along the trail. They followed the trail herds. The madams would bring them out from Omaha and Chicago and St. Paul; you would see them in Ogallala, and then again in Cheyenne or the Black Hills. But when the herds was all gone and the beef was shipped, the town was dead. The girls would go back where they came from and the gamblers would go with them."

A (Topeka) *Commonwealth* article noted that a Wichita dance hall exhibited an eclectic group of patrons: "The Texan, with mammoth spurs on his boots . . . is seen dancing by the side of a well-dressed, gentlemanly appearing stranger from some eastern city; both having painted and jeweled courtesans as partners."

Dance hall and saloon girls could earn money dancing or serving customers and nothing more, their primary job being to encourage liquor sales. Eddie Foy, vaudeville comedian and singer, spent two seasons in Dodge City and explains the women's duties in more detail: "Their profession may not appeal to the reader of today as having been a very moral one, but I want to say that many of those dance hall girls were personally as straight as a deaconess. I knew some who were widows, some married ones with worthless or missing husbands, and not a few of these had children. Of course, their family affairs were not made public. These girls were merely hired entertainers; their job was to dance with the men, talk to them, perhaps flirt with them a bit and induce them to buy drinks—no more. They pretended to drink with the men, but if a girl drank with every chap who bought for her, she would have been thoroughly soused and out of commission before the evening was over."

She didn't have on enough clothes to dust a fiddle.

The majority were prostitutes, however, utilizing the rooms above or behind the dance halls. "Crib" girls were at the very bottom of the caste system, making around 25 cents to $1 per client. Of course the dance hall owner received a cut of every transaction and even demanded rent for the crib, which could run $18 per week or $5 to $15 per day for a bedroom.

The brothels and upscale parlor houses offered clients a bit more in entertainment besides sex and liquor. Some offered multicourse meals along with exceptional dining companions. Not only lovely, these clever girls were cultured, captivating, and offered skills in other areas, such as dancing, singing, playing instruments, card playing, and intelligent conversation. The cost for their company went from $2 upwards to $35 for an all-night stay. Opulently decorated houses were usually owned by business-savvy madams who claimed 50 percent of each girl's hard-earned money. Bedrooms rented by the day or week, and any clothing or toiletry allowance must be paid back as well. Having the most beautiful and fashionable sporting women in town was good for business.

However, living in a dusty Cowtown during the summer heat posed a necessity for comfort rather than style, as Foy observed. "It was an eye-opener to me to discover that the women who entertained Dodge, no matter in what capacity, didn't as a rule dress in silks and satins, but in ginghams and cheap prints; and that goes for the dance hall girls when they were on duty, too."

His primpin' was shore hard on the soap supply an' stock water.

Recognizing a need to subdue complaints from the proper citizens, law enforcement and city councils moved red light districts away from the town centers. Kansas saloon keepers had to purchase annual licenses. Laws were imposed against lewd behavior, gambling, and disorderly conduct, having no intention of strict enforcement other than to collect fines. Town councils began taxing gamblers and prostitutes and enforcing fees on brothel owners.

Madams provided food, shelter, and a secure means of survival, yet the stories are tragic and unforgettable. Many are a testament to the hardiness and perseverance of surviving on the frontier, where men greatly outnumbered women.

One highly successful madam who faced the hand she'd been dealt was known as Squirrel Tooth Alice (Mary Elizabeth Haley Thompson), so named because of a gap in her front teeth and distinctly remembered because of her fondness for pet prairie dogs. She was kidnapped at a young age during a Comanche raid in Texas. Her family successfully paid the ransom to get her back, but she was kept locked away, ostracized by family and friends. An older male suitor offered his hand, but her father shot him. That's when "Libbie" left home as a young teen, falling in with a trail hand cowboy pushing a herd of cattle to Abilene, Kansas. Using her intelligence and perseverance, she went on to become a successful madam working in Kansas, Colorado, and Texas and raised nine children.

In spite of their fancy duds, most of the red-light gals had their hearts in the right place.

Squirrel Tooth Alice and her pet prairie dog

DROVERS COTTAGE

The boxlike structure rose three stories high and fronted the railroad tracks on the northeastern side of Abilene, Kansas. Built by Joseph McCoy for $15,000, it had thirty lavish, well-appointed rooms, a bar, a restaurant, and a gaming room. Patrons could enjoy the shade of the veranda that extended the length of one side while watching the arrival of the trains and activity of the stockyards to the west. The Drovers Cottage soon became the thriving center for the cattle trade.

The building was completed and fully furnished but did not open formally because a proprietor could not be hired. Finally, for the 1868 cattle season, James and Louisa Gore, a couple from St. Louis, filled the position.

The next year, the Gores leased the Cottage from McCoy for $1,000 a month. The establishment exchanged hands several times, including Gore himself as an owner, until Texas cattle dealer Moses B. George bought it in 1870. George added extensive renovations, increasing the rooms to one hundred and adding space for stabling up to fifty carriages and one hundred horses. The Gores remained in their position throughout the changes of ownership.

Wyatt Earp was known to have spent a lot of time at the poker tables at Drovers Cottage, solidifying his reputation as a skilled gambler. A longtime friend from Missouri of Marshal Wild Bill Hickok, Cole Younger brought other members of the James Gang to stay there. They kept a low profile for an entire week and reportedly robbed the surrounding towns but never Abilene.

When Abilene's city leaders declared their town to be done with the Texas cattle trade in early 1872, George struck a deal with Ellsworth businessmen. City leaders were anxious to welcome the trail bosses and cowmen diverted in

Drovers Cottage, Ellsworth, Kansas, relocated from Abilene
Kansas State Historical Society

their direction who needed reputable accommodations. In consideration of a $4,000 subsidy, George promised to have a hotel ready for business by the next season. He simply shipped the main structure of Abilene's Drovers Cottage by flatcar to Ellsworth and retained the Gores as managers; it was just as popular with the Texans as before.

Jim and Lou bought the Cottage back that next year, but they faced competition from the more elegant Grand Central Hotel. The end of the trailing days was drawing near. Gore was accused of setting fire to the Drovers Cottage on two different occasions in an effort to cover his losses. The second time, he spent a night in jail and the Gores were asked to leave Ellsworth. Returning to Abilene, the couple managed what was left of the original Drovers Cottage for another decade. An addition to the new courthouse in Abilene was later built on the former location of the famous hotel.

One of the star attractions at the Drovers Cottage was Mrs. Gore herself. Lou Gore established a reputation for providing the utmost care and concern for the trailing cowboys. Abilene cattleman and mayor Joseph McCoy recalled Mrs. Gore fondly: "From her earliest memory her home has been in a hotel, her father being to this day the proprietor of a large one at Niagara Falls. . . . Many a sick and wearied drover has she nursed and tenderly cared for until health was restored; or in the event of death soothed their dying moments with all the kind offices that a true sister only so well understands how to perform."

Lou's daughter was awarded an honorary lifetime membership in the Trail Drivers Association.

First Landlady in Abilene, Kansas

She took charge of the Drovers Cottage in the spring of '68 and conducted this Hotel for many years. In brief time it was learned that in the person of the new Landlady of the Cottage Hotel the Drovers had a true sympathetic friend and in their sickness a true guardian and nurse, one whose kind, motherly heart was ever ready to provide for every proper want, be they hungry, tired, thirsty or sick, it mattered not, she was the Florence Nightingale to relieve them. Many of the Old Trail Drivers remember Mrs. Gore and often speak of her as a most Noble Lady. Miss Margaret Gore, a daughter of Mrs. Lou Gore, is living at McPherson, Kansas. She was located last year through a letter written to Mrs. Amanda Burks of Cotulla, the Queen of the Old Trail Drivers' Association. Geo. W. Saunders, President of the Old Trail Drivers' Association, has been corresponding with Miss Gore. She has promised to attend our reunion November the 6th to 8th this Fall, 1924. President Saunders has made Miss Gore an honorary member of the Association for life out of respect of the memory of her most worthy Mother.

Working cowboy
Library of Congress

CHAPTER 7
COWTOWN REMEDIES

"It has been my pleasure of late years to visit some of the towns
and stations in Oklahoma, Kansas and Colorado where the old
Trail passed through in those early days, and the change that
meets your eyes is but little short of marvelous. Where saloons
and dance halls stood are now substantial school buildings and
magnificent churches, and the merry prattle of happy children is
heard on every corner. And it was a deep feeling of pride that came
to me, to know that I had had a humble part in bringing about this
wonderful change, which in a measure helped to settle the great
Northwest, which has proven so valuable an asset to our country."

J. J. (JOE) ROBERTS, TRAIL DRIVER

Air Baths

Directions:

Clothing is an artificial form of protection, tending to smother the skin and interfere with the elimination of waste matter through the pores. To take an air bath, simply remove the clothing in a comfortably warm room and allow the air to come in contact with the surface of the body.

Cure for Drunkenness, Guaranteed

A drachm is a small unit of volume equivalent to one-sixteenth of an ounce.

Ingredients:
11 drachms peppermint water
5 grains sulfate of iron
1 drachm spirit of nutmeg

Directions:

To be taken twice a day in doses of about a wineglassful or less, with or without water.

For Stomach Cramps

Ginger ale in a half glass of water in which a half teaspoon of soda has been dissolved.

A good cussing has more influence on a cowboy than good advice.

Cough Remedy

Ingredients:
½ pint brandy
¼ pound strained honey
2 drachms oil tar

Directions:

Dose: ½ teaspoon 3 times a day. Set the bottle into a kettle of cold water and let it heat over a hot stove. It is then ready for use. One drachm equals one eighth of an ounce.

Help for a Cough

Directions:

Get ground licorice root, and take a little on the point of a knife, as often as needed.

Earache

He was plumb weak north of his ears.

Directions:

Pour castor oil, or sweet oil, or British oil into ear.

Roast cabbage stalks and squeeze the juice into ear.

Warm a spoonful of urine and put a few drops into ear.

Chapped Lips

Directions:

Dissolve beeswax in a small quantity of sweet oil by heating carefully. Apply the salve 2–3 times a day, and avoid wetting the lips as much as possible.

Chapped Hands or Face

Directions:

Rub well in dry oatmeal after every washing, and be particular regarding the quality of soap. Cheap soap and hard water are the enemies of good skin. Castile soap and rainwater will sometimes cure without any other assistance.

Cucumber Lotion

Directions:

Good results may sometimes be secured with oily skins by rubbing with sliced cucumbers. The cucumber pulp also may be pounded in a bag, the juice strained through and applied to the skin two or three times a day.

Hand Lotion

Ingredients:
1 quart rainwater
1 tablespoon gum tragacanth
3 ounces bay rum
1 teaspoon carbolic acid
Juice of 3 lemons, strained
3 ounces glycerin

Directions:

Boil rainwater; cool. Dissolve Tragacanth in water for 3 days or until dissolved, then beat. Add rest of ingredients. Scent with perfume. (Gum tragacanth is dried sap from lockweed).

Them gals shore looked temptin' what with their
freshed-up spit-curls an' chalked noses.

Face Wash

Directions:

Either fresh milk or sour milk may be used for washing the face, with the very best results. Fresh cream is infinitely superior to any "cold cream" ever devised. Buttermilk makes a very good skin whitener in many cases for either face or hands.

Hair Lotion

Ingredients:

25 grains salicylic acid

75 grains borax

½ ounce tincture of cantharides (Spanish fly)

3 ounces bay rum

2 ounces rosewater

Water

He shore was considerably whiffy on the lee side.

Directions:

Mix above ingredients, adding enough clean water to make 8 ounces. Thorough and prolonged brushing of the hair night and morning will ensure its luxuriant growth.

Help for Weak Lungs

Directions:

For weak lungs take 1 pint brandy, ⅓ teacup of castor oil, 10 cents' worth of loaf sugar. Put on the stove, boil thoroughly and bottle. Use two or three times per day. The dose is 1 tablespoonful.

Itch

Directions:

Use sulfur and lard. Horse or human urine works, too. Anybody's will do.

Oatmeal Water

Directions:

Oatmeal boiled in water may be strained, using the liquid for wash. A little raw oatmeal stirred into cold water for washing the face is excellent for making the skin soft and smooth.

Red Face

Directions:

A red face, although usually accompanied by a thin-skinned condition, in most cases represents imperfect circulation. Outdoor life is advised. Frequent washing of the face with cold water will be beneficial.

Strawberry Lotion

Directions:

Strawberries were used by the ladies of ancient Rome to whiten the skin. Fresh, ripe strawberries should be mashed to a pulp and the juice strained through a cloth. Dilute with an equal part of water and a pinch of borax. This tends to whiten the skin and make it clear.

> After he comes out of the dippin' vat an' buys everything the barbers got, his own folks don't know him by sight or smell.

Toothpaste

Directions:

The teeth and gums should be carefully brushed after each meal with a medium soft brush. Using as a wash, mix equal parts alcohol, rosewater, and Listerine. (Listerine was invented by Dr. Joseph Lister as a surgical antiseptic.)

Toothache

Directions:

Make a small amount of wine from pokeberries and mix one part of the wine with eight parts white whiskey (unaged whiskey or moonshine). Take a small spoonful just a couple of times a day. It's also good for rheumatism and muscle cramps.

Painless Cure for Warts

Directions:

Drop a little vinegar on the wart and cover it immediately with cooking soda. Put on as much soda as you can pile on, and let it remain ten minutes. Repeat several times a day, and in three days, the wart will be gone. A good remedy for corns also.

Worms

Directions:

Eat tobacco seeds.

Eat a head of garlic every day until they're gone.

Put 3–4 drops of turpentine in a teaspoon of sugar and eat it.

Put some charcoal in a quart of water and drink it.

STOCKYARDS AND PACKING HOUSES

A group of investors purchased half a section of land in Cook County, Illinois, and built the Union Stockyards in 1865. That next spring, the first of the big herds hit the trail from Texas to train points in Kansas and then were transported by rail to Chicago. From the end of the Civil War to the 1920s, the Union Stockyards processed more meat than anywhere else in the world. The Kansas City Stockyard Company set up shop on the east bank of the Kaw River on one hundred acres, and by 1886 began hosting the American Royal Cattle Show. Packing houses and stockyards soon followed in other cities throughout the United States. Cleveland Union Stockyards Co. organized in 1881; Omaha's stockyards, covering more than 250 acres, opened in 1884; and the Union Stockyards of Peoria, Illinois, comprising

Fort Worth Stockyards Company, also known as "The Wall Street of the West"
Cattle Raisers Museum, Fort Worth, Texas

almost 35 acres in 1874, included a meat-packing plant and office space for livestock dealers, the press, loan companies, veterinarians, and government inspectors.

The trains arrived to Fort Worth in 1876. Pens, barns, and a new Livestock Exchange building were constructed at Fort Worth to house the livestock commission, telegraph and railroad offices, earning the title "The Wall Street of the West." Cowtown Coliseum was completed in 1907. By 1917 the Fort Worth Stockyards were the largest horse and mule market in the world. Oklahoma National Stockyards in Oklahoma City was organized on 120 acres in 1910 and is now the largest stocker/feeder cattle market in the world.

Chicago became the center of the meat packing industry for our country. Philip Armour and Gustavus Swift became two of the leading tycoons.

> The Peoria Union Stockyards were "sort of like a combined hotel, stock market and fruit and vegetable market all rolled into one."
>
> MILBURN CROSS,
> GENERAL MANAGER

Making link sausages—machines stuff 10 feet per second. Swift & Co.'s Packing House, Chicago, USA
Library of Congress

Gustavus F. Swift developed efforts to improve the elimination of waste in the meat packing industry. Originally from Cape Cod, his curiosity to operate more efficient butchering operations began while working in his brother's butcher shop at the age of fourteen. History has differing opinions on who coined the term "use everything of the hog but the squeal," but the majority concur that it fit Swift's philosophy of the business and credit is given to him. While running "the yards" in Chicago, he pioneered the use of animal by-products for many other products, such as glue, soap, and fertilizer.

In an effort to cut out the middleman, Swift even traveled west to negotiate shipments himself. To save on shrinkage of live cattle as they were transported east, he began to slaughter and dress the beef in Chicago and then perfected the ice-cooled train car to transport the meat to even more consumers.

Because of Swift's efforts in processing efficiency, refrigeration, and inspiring notable competition, meat prices spiraled downward as demand for beef and by-products increased. America became a beef-eating nation.

One-Two-Three-Four Cake

Directions:

One scant cup Cottolene; two cups sugar; three cups flour; four eggs.

Mix and bake the same as pound cake (350°F for about 1 hour).

As a replacement for lard, Cottolene was made from two by-products: cotton seed oil and beef tallow.

Ad for "Cottolene" cottonseed oil shortening, a product of the N. E. Fairbank Company
Library of Congress

In the opposite direction moving further west, one of the notable markets was the E. A. Tovrea and Co. butchery and stockyards in Phoenix, Arizona. It grew to an impressive complex known as the world's largest feedlot, processing up to 300,000 head every year. Opened in 1919 by cattleman Edward Ambrose Tovrea to support his sprawling cattle ranches, they operated under the principle that quality meats come from quality livestock.

The Arizona Packing Company processed beef, hogs, and sheep and sold cured meats. They also manufactured shortening made from cottonseed oil and beef tallow under the brand names of Fenix and Desert Bloom. An office complex added by Edward's son Phillip included space for a café. Built on-site, the saloon features a thirty-foot-long bar in intricately carved cherry mahogany. The Stockyards Restaurant opened in 1947 at the Tovrea packing house in Phoenix and became a popular gathering place for cattlemen, livestock buyers, and bankers. The restaurant remains and, according to owner Gary Lasko, continues to honor many of the same menu items. The building is now listed in the City of Phoenix Historical Register.

Stockyards café at Tovrea was rebuilt after a fire in 1954.
Gary Lasko

Sanford Ranch cowboys, Texas Panhandle
Natalie Bright

Of all the truths in the world, the cowboy is one of them.

DEVIL'S ROPE

Almost as soon as it began, it ended.

    The largest controlled migration of livestock the world has ever realized started with a string of "half-wild" Texas Longhorns. A skilled worker accepted the challenge, and the trail driving cowboy collided with frontier settlements that were willing to perfect a service industry and supply the demand. Enthusiasm for a new industry was ignited in a big way. The railroads' reach continued, and Michael Kelly in DeKalb, Illinois, twisted two pieces of wire together, calling it his "thorny fence." As with all good things that come to an end, Cowtowns disappeared into the realm of long-forgotten Western lore.

Corner post on barbed-wire fence; ranch near Marfa, Texas
Library of Congress

RECIPE INDEX

ACKNOWLEDGMENTS

Much thanks to Shirley and Don Creacy, who ran the Wild Cow Ranch Chuck Wagon Cooking Team for fourteen years, participating in cook-offs across the country and bringing home numerous awards. Their insight and expertise on this topic have proved vitally important. I appreciate the time Sue Cunningham took to talk to me about her recipes. She, along with her sister Jean Cates, cooked for the award-winning C-Bar-C Chuck Wagon, a skill they learned from helping their father. Thanks to the working cowboys and cowgirls who allowed me to photograph them at the Sanford Ranch. Their knowledge and love for what they do is inspiring. My sincerest appreciation goes to two dear friends and historians, Jane Little Botkin and Randi Samuelson-Brown, whose support, encouragement, and research tips kept me on track.

Many accounts about Cowtown omit information about the Indian Nation territory located between Texas and Kansas. I knew several authors who could help me. Thanks to Sarah Elisabeth Sawyer, Choctaw storyteller, author, and historian, for her insight, and inspirational author Carmen Peone, who brought a unique viewpoint from her life on a reservation in the Pacific Northwest.

Another vital resource for authors is the archival experts. I have been lucky to work with a few and want to thank the following for their efforts, interest, and willingness to help me with this project: Gabrielle Harris at Fort Worth Cattle Raisers Museum, Lisa Keys at Kansas State Historical Society, and Warren Stricker at Panhandle-Plains Historical Museum. Members of the American Chuck Wagon Association have proved extremely helpful. This group is dedicated to the preservation of the history of the chuck wagon.

Thanks to the TwoDot/Globe Pequot team for the opportunity and for your thoroughness and efforts on this project. Thank you, Tami Griffitt, for your input and extraordinary research skills. As always thanks to Chris, Casey, and David. Your support means the world. Even though I know they grow weary of my constant chatter about my book topics, they endure the taste testing and even help with research and reading pages when called upon, which allows me to keep doing what I love.

ABOUT THE AUTHOR

Natalie Bright is an award-winning author of twenty books for kids and adults, a writing instructor, a blogger, and a cattle ranch owner. She completed a BBA in business/marketing and enjoys hanging around chuck wagon events, exploring museums, and photographing all things Western. Natalie is a lifetime recipe and cookbook collector, and she loves bringing the fascinating history of eating to new generations of foodies. She is a member of Western Writers of America and Women Writing the West and was honored with a Lifetime Membership Award from Texas High Plains Writers. Her first book for TwoDot, *Keep 'Em Full and Keep 'Em Rollin': The All-American Chuck Wagon Cookbook*, won first place in the Will Rogers Medallion Awards for excellence in contributions to literature of the American West.